CHILD CUSTODY, VISITATION, AND SUPPORT IN PENNSYLVANIA

CHILD CUSTODY, VISITATION, AND SUPPORT IN PENNSYLVANIA

Rebecca A. DeSimone
Attorney at Law

SPHINX® PUBLISHING
AN IMPRINT OF SOURCEBOOKS, INC.®
NAPERVILLE, ILLINOIS
www.SphinxLegal.com

First Edition, 2002

Published by: Sphinx® Publishing, An Imprint of Sourcebooks, Inc.®

Naperville Office
P.O. Box 4410
Naperville, Illinois 60567-4410
630-961-3900
Fax: 630-961-2168
www.sourcebooks.com
www.SphinxLegal.com

This publication is designed to provide accurate and authoritative information in regard to the subject matter covered. It is sold with the understanding that the publisher is not engaged in rendering legal, accounting, or other professional service. If legal advice or other expert assistance is required, the services of a competent professional person should be sought.

From a Declaration of Principles Jointly Adopted by a Committee of the American Bar Association and a Committee of Publishers and Associations

This product is not a substitute for legal advice.

Disclaimer required by Texas statutes.

Library of Congress Cataloging-in-Publication Data
DeSimone, Rebecca A., 1963-
    Child custody, visitation, and support in Pennsylvania / Rebecca A. DeSimone.-- 1st ed.
        p. cm. -- (Legal survival guides)
Includes index.
    ISBN 1-57248-242-7 (alk. paper)
  1. Custody of children--Pennsylvania--Popular works. 2. Visitation rights (Domestic relations)--Pennsylvania--Popular works. 3. Child support--Law and legislation--Pennsylvania--Popular works. I. Title. II. Series
    KFP104.6.Z9 D47 2002
    346.74801'73--dc21
                                                                    2002026973

Printed and bound in the United States of America.

VHG Paperback — 10 9 8 7 6 5 4 3 2 1

CONTENTS

USING SELF-HELP LAW BOOKS

Before using a self-help law book, you should realize the advantages and disadvantages of doing your own legal work and understand the challenges and diligence that this requires.

THE GROWING
TREND

Rest assured that you won't be the first or only person handling your own legal matter. For example, in some states, more than seventy-five percent of divorces and other cases have at least one party representing him or herself. Because of the high cost of legal services, this is a major trend and many courts are struggling to make it easier for people to represent themselves. However, some courts are not happy with people who do not use attorneys and refuse to help them in any way. For some, the attitude is, "Go to the law library and figure it out for yourself."

We at Sphinx write and publish self-help law books to give people an alternative to the often complicated and confusing legal books found in most law libraries. We have made the explanations of the law as simple and easy to understand as possible. Of course, unlike an attorney advising an individual client, we cannot cover every conceivable possibility.

COST/VALUE
ANALYSIS

Whenever you shop for a product or service, you are faced with various levels of quality and price. In deciding what product or service to buy, you make a cost/value analysis on the basis of your willingness to pay and the quality you desire.

When buying a car, you decide whether you want transportation, comfort, status, or sex appeal. Accordingly, you decide among such choices as a Neon, a Lincoln, a Rolls Royce, or a Porsche. Before making a decision, you usually weigh the merits of each option against the cost.

When you get a headache, you can take a pain reliever (such as aspirin) or visit a medical specialist for a neurological examination. Given this choice, most people, of course, take a pain reliever, since it costs only pennies; whereas a medical examination costs hundreds of dollars and takes a lot of time. This is usually a logical choice because it is rare to need anything more than a pain reliever for a headache. But in some cases, a headache may indicate a brain tumor and failing to see a specialist right away can result in complications. Should everyone with a headache go to a specialist? Of course not, but people treating their own illnesses must realize that they are betting on the basis of their cost/value analysis of the situation. They are taking the most logical option.

The same cost/value analysis must be made when deciding to do one's own legal work. Many legal situations are very straight forward, requiring a simple form and no complicated analysis. Anyone with a little intelligence and a book of instructions can handle the matter without outside help.

But there is always the chance that complications are involved that only an attorney would notice. To simplify the law into a book like this, several legal cases often must be condensed into a single sentence or paragraph. Otherwise, the book would be several hundred pages long and too complicated for most people. However, this simplification necessarily leaves out many details and nuances that would apply to special or unusual situations. Also, there are many ways to interpret most legal questions. Your case may come before a judge who disagrees with the analysis of our authors.

Therefore, in deciding to use a self-help law book and to do your own legal work, you must realize that you are making a cost/value analysis. You have decided that the money you will save in doing it yourself outweighs the chance that your case will not turn out to your satisfaction. Most people handling their own simple legal matters never have a problem, but occasionally people find that it ended up costing them more to have an attorney straighten out the situation than it would have if they had hired an attorney in the beginning. Keep this in mind if you decide to handle your own case, and be sure to consult an attorney if you feel you might need further guidance.

LOCAL RULES   The next thing to remember is that a book that covers the law for the entire nation, or even for an entire state, cannot possibly include every procedural difference of every county court. Whenever possible, we provide the exact form needed; however, in some areas, each county, or even each judge, may require unique forms and procedures. In our *state* books, our forms usually cover the majority of counties in the state, or provide examples of the type of form that will be required. In our *national* books, our forms are sometimes even more general in nature but are designed to give a good idea of the type of form that will be needed in most locations. Nonetheless, keep in mind that your *state*, county, or judge may have a requirement, or use a form, that is not included in this book.

You should not necessarily expect to be able to get all of the information and resources you need solely from within the pages of this book. This book will serve as your guide, giving you specific information whenever possible and helping you to find out what else you will need to know. This is just like if you decided to build your own backyard deck. You might purchase a book on how to build decks. However, such a book would not include the building codes and permit requirements of every city, town, county, and township in the nation; nor would it include the lumber, nails, saws, hammers, and other materials and tools you would need to actually build the deck. You would use the book as your guide, and then do some work and research involving such matters as whether you need a permit of some kind, what type and grade of wood are available in your area, whether to use hand tools or power tools, and how to use those tools.

Before using the forms in a book like this, you should check with your court clerk to see if there are any local rules of which you should be aware, or local forms you will need to use. Often, such forms will require the same information as the forms in the book but are merely laid out differently, use slightly different language, or use different color paper so the clerks can easily find them. They will sometimes require additional information.

CHANGES IN THE LAW

Besides being subject to state and local rules and practices, the law is subject to change at any time. The courts and the legislatures of all fifty states are constantly revising the laws. It is possible that while you are reading this book, some aspect of the law is being changed or a court is interpreting a law in a different way. You should always check the most recent statutes, rules and regulations to see what, if any changes have been made.

In most cases, the change will be of minimal significance. A form will be redesigned, additional information will be required, or a waiting period will be extended. As a result, you might need to revise a form, file an extra form, or wait out a longer time period; these types of changes will not usually affect the outcome of your case. On the other hand, sometimes a major part of the law is changed, the entire law in a particular area is rewritten, or a case that was the basis of a central legal point is overruled. In such instances, your entire ability to pursue your case may be impaired.

Again, you should weigh the value of your case against the cost of an attorney and make a decision as to what you believe is in your best interest.

INTRODUCTION

Proceeding through a custody case and/or a support case is in all probability one of the most common, and most traumatic, encounters within the legal system. At a time when you are least likely to possess extra funds, paying a family lawyer can be one of the most expensive bills to pay. In a contested custody case, it is not uncommon for the parties to incur legal bills of over $10,000. Horror stories abound of lawyers charging substantial fees with only modest progress. This book is designed to assist you in understanding custody, support, and visitation issues to the extent that should you choose to retain the services of an attorney, you will be aware of that which is taking place in your case. You will have the knowledge to engage in meaningful discussions and discourse with your counsel. Further, you will not waste costly time in having your lawyer repeatedly explaining the basic aspects of the custody, support, or visitation process since you will have gained a comprehensive understanding and working knowledge of these basics in your thorough review of this book.

Although this book is designed to enable you to proceed through the custody, support, or visitation maze without the need to hire an attorney, it is recommended that you consider the complexities of these processes. It is generally unlikely that a layperson could proceed with ease through the intricacies of most custody, support, or visitation cases and thus we suggest using this book as a reference guide and a line of support in your particular situation.

To be sure, this is not a law school course. It is rather, a practical guide to move you through "the system" as easily as possible. Most of the legal terminology has been eliminated. For ease of understanding, this book uses the term spouse to refer to your husband or wife, your boyfriend or girlfriend, your mate or significant other, your live-in or co-habitant (whichever applies), and the terms child and children are used interchangeably. Gender selections have been made for ease of discussion and in no way are meant to suggest preference or standard. In most counties, custody cases are filed with the prothonotary's office. However, in some areas, such as Philadelphia County, custody cases are filed with the family court clerk's office. Throughout this book, we will use the word Prothonotary which will also mean Clerk for those counties with a clerk's office, unless otherwise indicated.

Please bear in mind that different judges, and courts in different counties, may have their own particular (if not wholly peculiar) procedures, forms, and ways of handling matters. The prothonotary's office (or family court clerk's office in those counties with a family court, such as Philadelphia) often can tell you if they have any special forms or requirements. Personnel at the prothonotary's office cannot give legal advice (they are not permitted to do so) however they can apprise you of what their court or judges require.

Section One of this book will provide to you with a comprehensive overview of the relevant area of law that is the focus of this book. Section Two will address the primary considerations of custody, as it relates to such areas as agreement standards, mediation, and paternity.

The focus of Section Three is visitation. Section Four discusses child support as it relates to eligibility, calculation, and enforcement.

Filing procedures and modifications of original orders are explained in Section Five. Section Six discusses the legal system of Pennsylvania and how to deal with attorneys.

A thorough glossary is included to help explain complex terms that are covered in this text. Finally, seven appendices complete the resources of the book.

Section 1: Preliminary Considerations

Marriage, Cohabitation, or Encounters

1

Several years (or perhaps only many months ago), you made a determination to get married, to cohabitate with your significant mate, or simply to engage in an encounter which ultimately resulted in a child or children. This chapter will discuss, in a very general manner, the basics of a marital union, cohabitation, or an altogether brief encounter.

Marriage

Marriage is frequently referred to as a contract. It is a legal contract, and, for many, it is also a religious contract. This book will deal only with the legal aspects. The wedding ceremony involves the bride and groom reciting certain vows that are actually mutual promises about the way in which they will treat each other. There are also legal papers signed, such as a marriage license and a marriage certificate. These formalities create certain rights and obligations for the husband and wife. Although the focus at the ceremony is on the emotional and romantic aspects of the relationship, the legal reality is that family rights are being created. Such rights and obligations must often be addressed through a legal proceeding when you and your "mate" have separated.

Marriage will give each of the parties certain rights in property, and it creates certain obligations with respect to the support of any children the parties have together (or adopt). Unfortunately, most people do not fully realize that these rights and obligations are being created until it comes time for a divorce, separation, or other departure from one another. Pennsylvania does recognize common law marriage (discussed next). Thus unions resulting in the birth of a child or children create certain specific rights and obligations. Pennsylvania does not, however, recognize homosexual marriage.

LEGAL SEPARATION

Since Pennsylvania is a common law marriage state (parties may tell people that they are husband and wife, and under certain circumstances, be deemed married without a marriage license, certificate, or ceremony), no law of legal separation exists. Pennsylvania does not permit a legal separation. This procedure is available in some states, and is used to divide the property and provide for child custody and support in cases where the husband and wife live separately, but remain married. This is usually used to break the financial rights and obligations of a couple whose religion does not permit divorce.

Some states refer to this procedure as "divorce from bed and board." It is an old procedure that is gradually fading from use. Pennsylvania does provide the ability to obtain child support or alimony, and determine custody and visitation rights, without getting a divorce, but it does not allow for the division of property. This procedure without divorce, often mistakenly called a legal separation, is beyond the scope of this book.

LEGAL DIVORCE

Legal divorce is the process of breaking your matrimonial bonds; the termination of your marriage contract and partnership. The stress created here is that of going through a court system procedure and having to deal with your spouse as you go through it. However, when compared to the other aspects of divorce, the legal divorce does not last as long. On the other hand, the legal divorce can be the most confrontational and emotionally explosive stage.

Generally, there are three matters to be resolved through the legal divorce process:

1. the divorce of two people, giving each the legal right to marry someone else;

2. the division of their property and responsibility for debts (called equitable distribution); and,

3. the care and custody of their children.

Although it is theoretically possible for the legal divorce to be concluded within months, the legalities may continue for years, mostly caused by the emotional aspects leading to battles over the children. Those issues are precisely the focus of this book.

CHILDREN AND DIVORCE

The effect upon your children, and your relationship with them, can often be the most painful and long-lasting aspect of divorce. Your relationship with your children may become strained as they work through their feelings of blame, guilt, disappointment, and anger. This strain may continue for many years. You and your children may even need professional counseling. Also, as long as there is child support and partial custody, shared custody, or visitation involved, you will be forced to have at least some contact with your ex-spouse.

ALTERNATIVES
TO DIVORCE

By the time you have purchased this book, and read this far, you have probably already decided that you want a divorce, a separation, or to disassociate from you mate. However, if what you have just read and thought about has made you want to make a last effort to save your marriage, there are a few things you can try. These are only very basic suggestions. Details, and other suggestions, can be offered by professional marriage counselors.

Talk to your spouse. Choose the right time (not when your spouse is trying to unwind after a day at work, or is trying to quiet a screaming baby) and talk about your problems. Try to establish a few ground rules for the discussion, such as:

- talking about how you feel, instead of making accusations that may start an argument;

- each person listening while the other speaks (no interrupting);

- each person saying something that he or she likes about the other, and about the relationship; or,

- each person discussing the importance of their child or children.

As you talk, you may want to discuss such things as where you would like your relationship to go, how it has changed since you got married, and what can be done to bring you closer together.

Counseling. Counseling is not the same as giving advice. A counselor should not be telling you what to do. A counselor's job is to assist you in figuring out what you really want to do. A counselor will ask questions that will get you thinking. Actually, just talking things out with your spouse is a form of self-counseling. The only problem is that it is difficult to remain objective and non-judgmental. Both of you need to be able to calmly analyze what the problems are, and discuss possible solutions.

Very few couples seem to be able to do this successfully, which is why there are professional marriage counselors. As with doctors and lawyers, good marriage counselors are best discovered by word of mouth. You may have friends who can direct you to someone who helped them. Also, you can check with your family doctor or with your clergyman for a referral, or even scan the telephone yellow pages under "Marriage and Family Counselors" or some similar category. You can see a counselor either alone or with your spouse. It may be a good idea for you to see a counselor even if you are going through with the divorce or separation. Family counselors may be helpful for the children as well if the children are age-appropriate for such services.

RESIDENCY 2

In order to be eligible to file for custody in Pennsylvania, either you or your spouse must be a resident of Pennsylvania for a period of at least six months immediately before filing.

It is important to distinguish between the terms resident and domiciliary. You are a resident of a state if you live in that state at least part of the time. You are a domiciliary of the state that you consider to be the primary and permanent state in which you live. A person may be a resident of more than one state, but may only be a domiciliary of one state. Read the following examples for a better understanding of these differences.

Example 1: You live seven months of the year in Florida and five months in Pennsylvania. You consider Florida to be the primary place you live, and use your Florida address for your voter registration, income tax returns, car registration, driver's license, and to receive most of your important mail. You are a domiciliary of Florida, and a resident of both Florida and Pennsylvania. You may file for custody in the Commonwealth of Pennsylvania, provided you have been a resident for at least the past six months.

Example 2: Your main home is in Princeton, New Jersey; but you also own a town home in Philadelphia because that is where you work. You typically spend Friday through Sunday in New Jersey and stay in Philadelphia the rest of the week. You consider New Jersey to be the primary place you live, and use your Princeton address for your voter registration, income tax returns, car registration, driver's license, and to receive most of your important mail. You are a domiciliary of New Jersey, a resident of both New Jersey and Pennsylvania. You may file for custody in the Commonwealth of Pennsylvania, provided you have been a resident for at least the past six months.

It is not necessary that you or your spouse have been physically in the Commonwealth of Pennsylvania for the entire six month period before filing, but only that the period of your residency began at least six months ago. For example, during the six month period you may leave Pennsylvania for business, visiting relatives, for a vacation, or to return to the state where you are domiciled; as long as you do not *abandon* your residence in Pennsylvania. Abandonment in the Commonwealth of Pennsylvania constitutes vacating your residence or domicile with the overt intention not to return. Intention not to return is determined by actions or conduct of the abandoning party. (Has he or she removed all of his or her belongings and personal effects? Has he or she informed you of the departure?)

Generally, residence will only become an issue if your spouse makes it one. There is no conclusive test that can be applied to decide whether a person is, or is not, a resident. In a dispute over residency, the judge will look at all the circumstances and determine whether you or your spouse meet the residency requirement.

Your custody case may be filed in the county where either of you reside. You could also file in any county that you both agree upon, provided the court in that county approves. However, there are few situations in which this would be practical (such as if you both will soon be moving to another county and want to be close to the court that will be handling your case).

> ***Warning:*** There are many problems that can arise in this situation, so if you think you may want to do this, you should consult an attorney in Pennsylvania and an attorney in the state where you intend to file for custody, visitation, or support. The information provided here is only for the purpose of making you aware of the possibility of filing in another state and to give you some basic information so that you can better discuss this option with an attorney.

To determine how long it takes to have your family matter addressed, you need to consider the residency requirement, any required separation period, any waiting period required by law, and the *backlog* of cases the court may have. A backlog of cases indicates that the court is extremely busy with many pending cases and as a result the court cannot easily address and handle the cases scheduled. Thus, the time frame for each case to be heard may be extended to accommodate for the heavy volume of cases pending before the court. You also need to be aware of how the laws of that state regarding child custody, visitation, and support differ from the laws of Pennsylvania.

YOUR SPOUSE OR MATE 3

You need to evaluate your situation with respect to your spouse. Have both of you already agreed to your child custody, visitation, or support arrangements? If not, what kind of reaction do you expect from your spouse? Your expected reaction can determine how you proceed. If he or she reacts in a rational manner, you can probably use the custody consent procedure. However, if you expect an extremely emotional, and possibly violent, reaction, you will need to take steps to protect yourself and your children. You will have to start out expecting to employ all necessary court procedures. Be sure to read the section in Chapter 13 on "Protecting Yourself and Your Children."

Unless you and your spouse have already discussed child custody, visitation, and support, you do not want your spouse to know that you are thinking about filing custody or support. This is a legal tactic, although it may not seem that way at first. If your spouse knows or suspects that you are planning to seek custody or support, he or she may take certain steps to prevent you from getting a fair result.

These steps may include taking your child out of the jurisdiction or withholding the child from you. So, do not let on until you have collected all of the information you will need and are about to file with the court, or until you are prepared to protect yourself or your children from violence

SECTION 2: CHILD CUSTODY

Types of Custody 4
and Standards

In domestic relations cases, there are various types of custody. Generally, a court will determine which parent will have physical or legal responsibility for the child(ren) and the manner in which such custody arrangement will be set forth. The sections that follow will provide an overview of the nature of custody and the forms which it may take.

Temporary Custody

De facto (in fact) custody refers to who actually has custody of the child at this time. In order to formalize custody before you begin going to court, one should file a motion for *Pendente Lite* (pending litigation) or temporary custody. (see form 6, p.209.) Temporary custody will be reviewed based on the "best interests" of the child standard, to be discussed later. It is not an "initial" award of custody because it is understood to be temporary pending a full hearing. In order to be awarded temporary custody you must file a request for hearing and an order for temporary custody and support along with your Complaint for Custody or Divorce.

Sole/Primary Custody

Custody is made up of: legal custody and physical custody. A person with legal custody has the right to make long range plans and decisions for the:

- education;

- religious training;

- discipline,

- non-emergency medical care; and,

- other matters of major significance concerning the child's welfare.

A person with physical custody has the child living primarily with them and they have the right to make decisions as to the child's everyday needs. Sole custody is when both legal and physical custody are given to one parent.

NOTE: *The child can only have one primary residence.*

Split Custody

Split custody is easiest to describe in a situation where there are two children and each parent obtains full physical custody over one child. Some of the considerations that may bring about this result are age of the children and child preference.

Joint/Shared Custody

Courts in the Commonwealth prefer joint or shared custody. It is actually broken down into three categories. The first category is joint legal custody. It is where the parents share care and control of the upbringing of the child, but the child has only one primary residence. In shared physical custody, the second category, the child has two residences, spending at least 35% of his or her time with the other parent. Additionally, the third category is where you can make your own special joint custody agreement that is any combination of shared physical and joint legal custody. One example of this is when there is one residence for the child and the parents live with the child there on a rotating basis.

In order to assure the best interests of the child, the court looks very closely at joint custody agreements. The most important factor to joint legal custody that is also very relevant to shared physical custody is the ability of the parents to talk about and reach joint decisions that affect the child's welfare. If you are constantly fighting over what religion or what school, the court may strike down your agreement.

Other factors include:

- willingness to share custody;

- fitness;

- the child's relationships with parents;

- the child's preference;

- ability to stabilize the child's school and social life;

- closeness to parent's homes (primarily a factor during the school year) ;

- employment considerations (e.g. long hours, extensive travel, etc.);

- age and number of children;

- financial status; or,

- benefit to the parent.

Additionally, the sincerity of the parties involved is important. The court will want to make sure that joint custody isn't being traded for concessions on other points.

Another consideration is whether the grant of joint custody will affect any assistance programs. Currently, medical assistance is affected based on the award of joint legal custody. Be sure to check with your contact at any social service agencies before entering into an agreement or you may be jeopardizing your benefits. If a custody order is entered in your favor, the time allotment as to which parent has more time with the child(ren) may benefit you. However, if this happens, you may be entitled to receive an award of child support since you are caring for the children during the majority of the time. Your child support benefit may cause your existing medical assistance or welfare situation to be reduced since you would be receiving compensation from your former spouse rather than from the Commonwealth.

NOTE: *This list is not meant to be exhaustive and the courts will hear anything that they believe to be relevant.*

GRANDPARENTS OR OTHER RELATIVES

Generally, the natural parents will have a *presumptive* right to custody. That means that the law gives them custody unless someone tries to argue why the parents should not have it. Only in cases where the parents are found to be unfit, or there are exceptional circumstances, where third parties be granted custody. The legal presumption favoring a parent over a non-parent is a strong one, but can be argued against with clear and convincing evidence of certain factors such as

- parental unfitness;

- abandonment; or,

- intentional surrender (a parent gives up a child).

At any time after a divorce, grandparents may petition the court for visitation rights. Grandparents are consistently seeking a court-ordered period of visitation or time with their grandchild(ren) in situations in which one or both of the natural parents refuse to involve or include the grandparents in the lives of the child(ren). The Commonwealth of Pennsylvania recognizes grandparents rights. Upon a showing of evidence that supports a meaningful and healthy connection with the grandparent or grandchild relationship, the court will generally award a period of time to the grandparents if such time is found to be in the best interests of the child(ren).

THE BEST INTERESTS OF THE CHILD

Regardless of any agreement you may have reached, the court's standard for initially awarding custody is to determine the *best interests of the child*. In order to do this they look at several factors. It is important to remember, though, that no one factor carries any more weight than any other. The following is some of the factors (but not all) that courts will consider.

PRIMARY CARE GIVER

The primary care giver is the person who takes care of the child, feeds the child, shops for his or her clothes, gets them up for school, bathes them, and arranges day care. This is generally the person the child turns to when he or she gets hurt.

FITNESS

Fitness addresses the psychological and physical capacities of the parties seeking custody. The court may also consider evidence of abuse by a party against the other parent, the party's spouse, or any child residing within the party's household (including another child).

CHARACTER AND REPUTATION

This focuses on what specific issues of character of the parent may impact upon his or her ability to properly care for the child.

AGREEMENTS	If there is already a custody agreement drafted, the court will definitely consider it. At some point, this is what you and the other parent have come up with, and the court will try to resolve those issues you do not agree.
ABILITY TO MAINTAIN FAMILY RELATIONSHIPS	Who will be able to keep the child's family most intact? Who is going to let the child speak with their ex-mother-in-law, for example? Who will not penalize the child for any adverse action on the part of the other parent? These are the questions the court will ask when considering the best interests of the child. Most courts believe that a child needs his or her extended family relationships, especially at a time when his or her parents are separating
CHILD PREFERENCE	The decision of the court may be reversed if it fails to hear the child's preference. However, the court has the discretion to interview the child out of the parents' presence. A child as young as 5 or 6 years of age may be heard. Though it is rare the court will hear from a child under 7 years, the child's ability to tell the truth from fiction, and maturity will be the guidelines for whether a child may be heard. A child of 10 or 12 years of age is certainly entitled to have his or her opinions heard and given weight in legal proceedings about custody. Additionally, the court has the power to appoint an attorney for the child in contested cases (those cases not agreed upon and disputed).
MATERIAL OPPORTUNITY	Which parent has the financial resources to give the child more things is given some weight in this decision as well.
AGE, HEALTH, AND GENDER OF CHILD	Any issues such as tender age of the child, health, or gender effect the welfare and best interests in placing the child with one parent over the other. The court will address each one separately.
OPPORTUNITY FOR VISITATION	How close do the parents live to each other? How close do they live to members of the child's extended family? Which parent lives closest to the child's school and social circle? It is important that the child's life is disrupted as little as possible. The parent that can afford the child more access to those activities and people he or she is used to will be given slightly more consideration.

LENGTH OF SEPARATION	How long have the parties been separated and what has the effect been upon the child plays a role as well.
ABANDONMENT	Is there a history of one parent walking out and leaving the other parent to cope with the child and the home? Which parent left when you last broke up? These issues weigh in part to show which parent will be best-suited to make it through rougher times with the child, and to demonstrate a stable home.
RELIGIOUS VIEWS	These will bear on the court's decision only if shown to affect the physical or emotional well being of the child. If one parent, for example, is religiously opposed to medical care, that parent may have a disadvantage in this decision.

CHILD CUSTODY PROCEDURE 5

This chapter will make clear the way in which child custody issues will be addressed and resolved. By applying the information contained within this chapter to your circumstances, you will obtain an idea of what to expect if the judge must decide these matters. If you and your spouse are trying to reach an agreement on these matters, this chapter will assist you in determining whether a custody proposal is sensible and even-handed.

As you have by now recognized through your review and reading of this book, Pennsylvania's Common Pleas Courts maintain jurisdiction over matters of family law such as divorce, property division, alimony, child custody, paternity, protection from abuse (PFA), child support, and spousal support. While most of these cases originate in the prothonotary's office, child custody, visitation, and support matters are handled through the Domestic Relations Section of the Common Pleas Court. Each of the Commonwealth's sixty-seven (67) counties has a Domestic Relations Section. You may locate the Domestic Relations Section of the Common Pleas Court in your area by looking in the blue pages of your local telephone book.

CHILD CUSTODY OVERVIEW

The decision to live apart is a difficult one for anyone, however it is most painful when children are involved in the family separation. Children have no part in the parent's determination to live separately. However, when parents do split, it has enormous effect upon their young lives. Children feel torn questioning the proper way in which to show affection to both parents when they are no longer together as a family. Despite the end of a couple's relationship, a mother and father have an undeniable responsibility and duty to continue to care for and make decisions that directly affect their children. The parents' choice in these decisions will ultimately manifest itself through the children's behavior, stability, and confidence about himself or herself. Although the couple's relationship may terminate, both the mother and father will continue to be parents.

OBTAINING
CUSTODY

Either one of the separated parents may petition the court for custody of a child. If the parties cannot agree about who should have custody, the court will grant custody either solely to one of the parents or joint custody to both of the parents.

Jurisdiction lies with the juvenile and domestic relations court to interpret the provisions of separation agreements relating to custody or visitation. Jurisdiction is the authority established by the court to try cases and rule upon legal matters within a particular geographic area. Jurisdiction also pertains to certain types of cases that may be heard by specific levels of courts, which deal only with that particular kind of case or controversy. If the agreement has been incorporated into a circuit court decree, the circuit court retains that jurisdiction.

FATHERS

In Pennsylvania, fathers can gain custody of their children. The law no longer favors one parent over the other. The parent seeking custody must meet the same criteria: what is in the best interests of the child.

A CHILD'S
INPUT

Courts will sometimes listen to the wishes of older children, however the preference of the child is not binding on the court. Courts rarely take into account the wishes of very young children.

CUSTODY
CONCILIATION
OFFICE

The central focus of the Custody Conciliation Office as it exists in its capacity as an arm of the Domestic Relations Section is to aid parents in structuring certain terms of their shared custody arrangement by creating a binding legal document. The Custody Office in your area provides a non-threatening, non-adversarial mediation session in which both parties are encouraged to negotiate and communicate their goals for parenting (such as structured partial custody times with each parent) through the assistance of a neutral third party, called a conciliator.

The process of conciliation involves varying levels of parental communication. Several steps in the custody process are put in place to provide parents with every opportunity to fashion an arrangement to which they may be firmly committed. It is obvious that a schedule you develop on your own, and not one that is imposed upon you by the court, will be one that you will more comfortably find acceptable. Thus, the purpose of the Custody Conciliators and the goal of the custody conferences is not to assess who may be the better parent, but rather to assist in preserving and maintaining the indispensable bond and relationship your children are entitled to experience with both parents.

The first step in the Custody Conciliation process involves both parents attending a four-hour seminar entitled, "Children Cope with Divorce" or some similarly titled program. Generally, there is a small cost for the program and your attendance is *mandatory* if either of you are involved in a divorce or custody proceeding.

Certain of the program's objectives include:

- examining the experience of separation and divorce from the children's perspective;

- exchanging certain skills, which parents may utilize to support the children's adjustment to the separation; and,

- discussing the manner by which to avoid placing children in a no-win situation with parents.

Custody Agreements

If you and the other parent have already come to a fair agreement on the custody and visitation issue, you may want to write your own stipulation and consent order. A stipulation is a statement of the settlement that you have reached. It is accompanied by a consent order for the judge to give the agreement the power of a court decision.

If you choose to go this route, you and the other parent should be as specific as you can to avoid future conflicts. Address such issues as:

- Who has legal custody?

- Which holiday does the child spend with you?

- What time and where may the other parent pick the child up?

- What time should the child be returned home?

- What is the procedure to follow if either of you are running late and won't be there on time?

- How much notice should you be given if they are planning a vacation?

- How far away may the other spouse move?

What you might think you can figure out as you go along could actually blow up into a full scale war later. The stipulations should state everything that you have agreed upon. You should not rely on any oral promises. If you both agreed on it, write it down (no matter how trivial it may seem now). Additionally, you should be sure to read this full section before proceeding in order to avoid having your stipulation and consent order ignored by the court or giving away rights of which you were unaware.

CONSENT CUSTODY ORDER

If both parents are in agreement regarding their shared custody arrangements, and they wish to have that agreement formalized into an Order of Court, both parents must appear voluntarily for a custody conference. Both parents must also have attended the four-hour "Children Cope with Divorce" seminar mentioned earlier. At this conference level, the conciliator puts into writing all of the terms you as the parties agree to, and provides you with the required documentation to obtain a *docket number* to have your agreement entered as a court order. A docket number is a number assigned for reference to your case on the court calendar. You should refer to this number on all of your communications or filings with the court. There is a filing fee for this process and you should check with your court's Domestic Relations Section for the cost in your area.

Even though both parents may have verbally agreed to certain custody arrangements, and both have already been functioning without these arrangements reduced to writing, it is highly recommended that you seek a formal Order of Court. The Order of Court will serve as a fall-back document, or a guide, whenever potential disagreements as to custody arrangements may occur (and they usually do.)

FILING A CUSTODY COMPLAINT

Should no agreement exist as to the terms of your custody arrangement, or if either party refuses to meet at a voluntary Custody Conciliation Conference, then you must proceed by petitioning the court for a Custody Order. A court petition takes the form of a Complaint. As is the case with all custody situations, each party must appear at an intake conference and each must attend the "Children Cope with Divorce" seminar. The form for filing a TEMPORARY CUSTODY COMPLAINT is on page 209 of this book. Should you not wish to file your own Complaint, an attorney may prepare and file one on your behalf.

NOTE: *For the purposes of this book, a Custody Complaint and a Temporary Custody Complaint are the same. Petition is another name for complaint.*

THE CUSTODY INTAKE CONFERENCE

A Custody Intake Conference will be scheduled once you have completed the "Children Cope with Divorce" seminar. The conference is an informal session, not a hearing. Therefore, no evidence or testimony is formally presented. The children are not to be present nor are they interviewed. There is no third party (for example, a friend of the family or a grandparent) to be present in the conference. Although it is not necessary for your attorney to be present during a custody conference, it is recommended that you seriously discuss with your counsel the potential benefit of having him or her present at the conference to represent you.

The custody conference provides a forum for you to present information about what is best for you and your children. It is not the court's goal to interfere or dictate personal decisions unless compelled to do so because the parties are ultimately unable to fashion a workable custody arrangement. Thus, at the custody conciliation conference, areas of agreement and disagreement are highlighted and the parties have the opportunity to smooth out points of contention and fashion an arrangement for custody with the assistance of the Custody Conciliation Supervisor.

Holidays/Summer Vacations/School Breaks/Birthdays are typically addressed at the Custody Conciliation Conference level. The Custody Conciliation Supervisor will attempt to fashion an Order which reflects the work schedules of both parents as well as availabilities of the parents which best suit the stated needs of all involved. With this fact in mind, the Conciliation Supervisor will discuss the holidays, both festive (such as Christmas, Easter, and Thanksgiving) and non-festive (such as Memorial Day, Independence Day, and Labor Day). The Custody Conciliation Supervisor will further set aside time for the child(ren) to be with the mother on Mother's Day and with the father on Father's Day. On birthdays, the children will generally be that parent who is celebrating a birthday. On the child(ren's) birthday(s), each parent usually spends a portion of the day with the respective child. Of course, this arrangement would not apply if considerable distance is involved in transporting the child(ren). The Custody Conciliation Supervisor will then attempt to fashion a Custody Order which takes distance into account and thereby provides blocks of time to each parent. This can be well set out during summer months when the child(ren) are out of school. Keep in mind there are as many ways to design and draft a Custody Order as there are different life stories. If the parents are flexible and communicate well, the custody process will be better effectuated.

CUSTODY
ORDERS

Custody orders are as different and varied as are individuals. Each order is crafted and developed based upon an examination of each couple's circumstance. You are the best person to make the determination as to the needs of your children and your lifestyles. Once the terms of your agreement are reduced to writing, they will be formalized into an Order of Court and signed by the Family Court Judge. Truly, most matters are resolved at this level. However, if complete agreement on the custody terms cannot be reached at this stage, you will then be scheduled to attend a conciliation conference. In the meantime, a Temporary Order of Court will be put in place and you must obey that order until the second conference. The goal of the Temporary Order of Court is to make certain that no breach in contact or communication between the children and both parents occurs until such time that a more permanent arrangement can be finalized.

The goal of the custody conciliation conference (custody intake) is to encourage agreement between the parties in such manner that both will be committed to a custody arrangement that will be formalized as a Court Order. The conciliator will assist the parties in reaching an agreement utilizing skills and methods employed in mediation. This conference, as was the last intake session, is also informal. There are no records of this proceeding and no evidence or testimony is permitted to be presented. Once again, although it is not necessary for your attorney to be present during a custody conference, it is recommended that you seriously discuss with your counsel potential benefit of having him or her present at the conference to represent you.

The custody conciliation conference may take several hours in an effort to resolve the issues and to fashion the terms of your Custody Agreement. If no agreement is reached, the Custody Conciliator will issue a Recommended Order and forward it to the court for the judge's signature. You must follow this order.

If you object to the Recommended Order, you must file a Request for an Adversarial Hearing within ten days from the date of the Order. Your matter will then be scheduled for a trial before the family court judge. You will be notified of the trial date and also of the date of a pre-trial conference which you, or your attorney on your behalf, must attend prior to the scheduled trial.

DIVORCE BATTLES OVER CUSTODY 6

In a divorce matter, generally, if you are the wife, the odds start out in favor of you getting custody. Do not depend solely upon the odds. Begin by reviewing the guidelines in this chapter on page 36. The judge will utilize many of these to determine the custody matter. For each item listed in that section, write down an explanation of the way in which that item applies to you. This will bolster your argument when you have your custody hearing with the judge or Custody Conciliator.

Child custody tends to be something that cannot be negotiated in a divorce. It is more often used as a threat by one of the parties in order to get something else, such as more of the property, or lower child support. If the essential issue is one of these other matters, do not be alarmed by a threat of a custody battle. In such cases, the other party probably does not truly wish to possess custody. If the critical issue is custody, you will not be able to negotiate for it, and, ultimately the judge or Custody Conciliator will decide the matter in any case.

MORAL FITNESS

Many custody conflicts center upon the moral fitness of one or both of the parents. If you become involved in this sort of a custody battle, you should hire a lawyer. Allegations of moral unfitness (such as illegal drug use, child abuse, or immoral sexual conduct) can require lengthy court hearings involving the testimony of many witnesses, presentation of evidence, as well as the possible need to employ a private investigator. For such a hearing, you will have need of the help of an attorney who knows the law, knows the right questions to ask of witnesses, and is skilled with the rules of evidence.

MAIN CAREGIVER

However, if the only question is whether you or your spouse have been the main caretaker of the child, you can always have friends, neighbors, and relatives attend court hearings (if they are willing to assist you) to testify on your behalf and it may not be necessary for you to have an attorney. However, should you have a need to subpoena unwilling witnesses to testify, you should have an attorney.

NOTE: *Witnesses are not permitted to be present in the Custody Conciliation rooms during the custody intake or conciliation process. You may have witnesses testify only when the conciliation process results in an impasse and a court hearing must take place.*

AGREEING ON CUSTODY

As with everything else in a custody matter, situations are ideal when both parties can agree on the question of custody of the children. Generally, the judge will accept any agreement you reach, provided it does not appear that your agreement will cause harm to your children. With respect to child custody, the Pennsylvania law makes it clear that the primary interest of the court is to protect and provide for the best interests of the child.

PUBLIC POLICY AND THE JUDGE'S DECISION

It is the official public policy of Pennsylvania to assure that each minor child has frequent and continuing contact with both parents after the parents separate or the marriage of the parties is dissolved, and to encourage parents to share the rights and responsibilities of child rearing. After considering all relevant facts, the father of the child will be given the same consideration as the mother in determining the primary residence of a child, irrespective of the age or sex of the child. Primary residence is defined as the principal home or dwelling of the child(ren).

In spite of this modern philosophy voiced by Pennsylvania (and many other states), you may find that many judges believe that (all things being equal) a young child is better off with the mother. Because of these statements in the law, a judge may go to great lengths to find that all things are not equal, thus justifying a decision to award custody to the mother. This occurs frequently throughout many states and the Commonwealth of Pennsylvania, and it is a reality you may have to face. To be fair, however, more cases than ever before show fathers being awarded significant custodial rights.

ORDERING SHARED CUSTODY

The practice in Pennsylvania law is for the court to order that the parental responsibility for a minor child be shared by both parents, unless the court finds that shared parental responsibility would be detrimental to the child. This indicates that, in most cases, the courts favors what is commonly known as shared custody or joint (partial) custody. However, very few parents can put aside their anger at each other to agree on what is best for their child. Shared custody may lead to more fighting. If shared custody is ordered, the child may still have a primary residence. In many cases in which custody is equally shared, no primary residence is required except for the purpose of school information.

If you and your spouse cannot agree upon how these matters will be handled, you will be leaving this important decision up to the judge. The judge cannot possibly know your child as well as you and your spouse, so does it makes sense for you to work this out yourselves.

FACTORS FOR THE JUDGE'S DECISION

If the judge must decide the question, he or she will consider the following factors:

- which parent is most likely to encourage and allow frequent and continuing contact with the other parent.

   NOTE: *The Pennsylvania Custody Statutes require the judge to consider this factor. (Pa. Cons. Stat. Ann. Tit. 23, Sec. 5301.)Although the above factors are not set forth in the custody statute, applicable case law requires the judge to consider them when making a Custody decision.*

- the love, affection, and other emotional ties existing between the child and each parent;

- the ability and willingness of each parent to provide the child with food, clothing, medical care, and other material needs;

- the length of time the child has lived with either parent in a stable environment;

- the permanence, as a family unit, of the proposed custodial home;

- the moral fitness of each parent;

- the mental and physical health of each parent;

- the home, school, and community record of the child;

- the age of the child or special needs of the child, and which parent is most able to attend to those needs; or

- any other fact the judge decides is relevant.

Unfit Parents

It is difficult to predict the outcome of a custody battle. There are too many factors and individual circumstances to make such a guess. The only exception is where one parent is clearly unfit and the other can prove it. The most common charges against a spouse are drug, physical, or sexual abuse. However, unless there has been an arrest and conviction, it is difficult to prove. In general, do not charge your spouse with being unfit unless you can prove it. Judges are not impressed with unfounded allegations, and such charges often do more harm that good.

Child's Preference

If your children are older (not infants), it may be a good idea to seriously consider their preference for with whom they would like to live. Your "fairness" and respect for their wishes may benefit you in the long run. Just be sure that you keep in close contact with them and visit them often. Knowing their preference may assist you in voicing your position, but keep in mind that the children's preference generally is not considered by Pennsylvania courts in making custody determinations.

MEDIATION

If you and your spouse are having trouble reaching an agreement, you should consider mediation. You may have heard the term mediator used in news reports about labor negotiations or the 1994 baseball strike. A mediator specializes in helping people reach an agreement that is fair and will last. The sessions are confidential and are not reported to the court. A mediator's role may be limited to custody or may also cover other issues such as marital property if you choose. Mediation is not an option that is appropriate in cases where there is a genuine issue of physical or sexual abuse of the child or one of the parties. It is also important to get a legal advisor for this process. The mediator's role is not to take sides, but to bring the two sides together. Additionally, if the mediator is not an attorney, he/she may be unaware of some specific legal issues.

PATERNITY 7

If the parents are unmarried, the child is the child of his/her mother. In order for the father to assert rights to the child (including rights to custody or visitation), paternity must be admitted or established in court. Paternity can be established by:

- judicial determination of paternity;

- father's acknowledgment of paternity in writing;

- father's open and *notorious* (known through reputation and in the community) recognition of the child as his own; or,

- by marrying the mother and then acknowledging himself as the father, either in writing or orally.

In order for a father to bring suit to establish paternity by judicial determination, he should file an action for "filiation"; but, this is not required to seek custody if any of the other three methods has established paternity. Once paternity is established, neither party will be given a preference based solely on the gender.

RAISING PATERNITY DOUBTS

One of the strongest presumptions in the law is that the child of a married woman is a child of her marriage. A husband of such a woman can only prove that he is not the father by proving that he had no access to his wife during the time of conception or that he was sterile. His evidence must be very persuasive and "clear and convincing" to the Court.

Raising paternity doubts is a support defense. However, openly admitting paternity and supporting the child can waive the defense.

UNMARRIED COHABITANTS

If the parents are unmarried, the child is the child of his or her mother. A father must assert his rights by establishing paternity as described at the beginning of the chapter. The Pennsylvania Statutes address paternity and the requirements to establish paternity as follows:

Section 5103. Acknowledgment and claim of paternity

(a) **Acknowledgment of paternity** —The father of a child born to an unmarried woman may file with the Department of Public Welfare, on forms prescribed by subsection (c), an acknowledgment of paternity of the child which shall include the consent of the mother of the child, supported by her affidavit. In such case, the father shall have all the rights and duties as to the child which he would have had if he had been married to the mother at the time of the birth of the child, and the child shall have all the rights and duties as to the father which the child would have had if the father had been married to the mother at the time of birth.

(b) Claim of paternity—If the mother of the child fails or refuses to join in the acknowledgment of paternity provided for in subsection (a), the Department of Public Welfare shall index it as a claim of paternity. The filing and indexing of a claim of paternity shall not confer upon the putative father any rights as to the child except that the putative father shall be entitled to notice of any proceeding brought to terminate any parental rights as to the child.

(c) Duty of hospital or birthing center—Upon the birth of a child to an unmarried woman, an agent of the hospital or birthing center where the birth occurred shall:

Provide the newborn's birth parents with an opportunity to complete an affidavit acknowledging paternity. The completed, signed and notarized affidavit shall be sent to the Department of Public Welfare. A copy shall be given to each of the birth parents. This affidavit shall contain:

(i) A sworn, signed statement by the birth mother consenting to the assertion of paternity.

(ii) A signed, notarized statement by the birth father acknowledging his paternity.

(iii) A written explanation of the parental duties and parental rights which arise from signing such a statement.

(iv) The Social Security numbers and addresses of both birth parents.

Provide written information, furnished by the Department of Public Welfare to the birth mother, which explains the benefits of having the child's paternity established, the availability of paternity establishment services and the availability of child support enforcement agencies.

(d) Conclusive evidence—An acknowledgment of paternity shall constitute conclusive evidence of paternity in any action to establish support. An acknowledgment of paternity may be set aside by the court only upon clear and convincing evidence that the defendant was unaware of the fact that he was acknowledging paternity when the acknowledgment was signed.

(e) Transfer —The Department of Health shall transfer to the Department of Public Welfare all acknowledgments or claims of paternity filed with the Department of Health under prior statutes.

(f) Certifications —The Department of Public Welfare shall provide necessary certifications under Part III (relating to adoption) as to whether any acknowledgment or claim of paternity has been filed in regard to any child who is a prospective adoptive child.

Section 5104. Blood tests to determine paternity

(a) Short title of section —This section shall be known and may be cited as the Uniform Act on Blood Tests to Determine Paternity.

(b) Scope of section —

Civil matters —This section shall apply to all civil matters.

Criminal proceedings —This section shall apply to all criminal proceedings subject to the following limitations and provisions:
(i) An order for the tests shall be made only upon application of a party or on the initiative of the court.

(ii) The compensation of the experts shall be paid by the party requesting the blood test or by the county, as the court shall direct.

(iii) The court may direct a verdict of acquittal upon the conclusions of all the experts under subsection (f). Otherwise, the case shall be submitted for determination upon all the evidence.

(iv) The refusal of a defendant to submit to the tests may not be used in evidence against the defendant.

(c) **Authority for test** —In any matter subject to this section in which paternity, parentage or identity of a child is a relevant fact, the court, upon its own initiative or upon suggestion made by or on behalf of any person whose blood is involved, may or, upon motion of any party to the action made at a time so as not to delay the proceedings unduly, shall order the mother, child and alleged father to submit to blood tests. If any party refuses to submit to the tests, the court may resolve the question of paternity, parentage or identity of a child against the party or enforce its order if the rights of others and the interests of justice so require.

(d) **Selection of experts.**—The tests shall be made by experts qualified as examiners of blood types, who shall be appointed by the court. The experts shall be called by the court as witnesses to testify to their findings and shall be subject to cross-examination by the parties. Any party or person at whose suggestion the tests have been ordered may demand that other experts qualified as examiners of blood types perform independent tests under order of court, the results of which may be offered in evidence. The number and qualifications of experts shall be determined by the court.

(e) **Compensation of experts**—The compensation of each expert witness appointed by the court shall be fixed at a reasonable amount. It shall be paid as the court shall order. Subject to general rules, the court may order that it be paid by the parties in such proportions and at such times as it shall prescribe or that the proportion of any party be paid by the county and that, after payment by the parties or the county, or both, all or part or none of it be taxed as costs in the action. Subject to general rules, the fee of an expert witness called by a party but not appointed by the court shall be paid by the party calling him, but shall not be taxed as costs in the action.

(f) Effect of test results —If the court finds that the conclusions of all the experts as disclosed by the evidence based upon the tests are that the alleged father is not the father of the child, the question of paternity, parentage or identity of a child shall be resolved accordingly. If the experts disagree in their findings or conclusions, the question shall be submitted upon all the evidence.

(g) Effect on presumption of legitimacy—The presumption of legitimacy of a child born during wedlock is overcome if the court finds that the conclusions of all the experts as disclosed by the evidence based upon the tests show that the husband is not the father of the child.

PATERNITY PROCESS

If the action seeks support for a child born out of wedlock and the alleged father is named as defendant, the defendant may acknowledge paternity in a verified writing. The conference officer shall advise the parties that pursuant to Section 5103(d) of Title 23 of the Pennsylvania Consolidated Statutes an acknowledgment constitutes conclusive evidence of defendant's paternity without further judicial ratification in any action to establish support. Upon defendant's execution of the written acknowledgment, the action shall proceed as in other actions for support.

If the defendant appears but does not execute an acknowledgment of paternity at the conference:

- The court shall enter an order directing the parties to appear for genetic testing. The order must advise the defendant that his failure to appear for the testing will result in entry of an order finding that he is the father of the child. The order must also advise the plaintiff that her failure to appear for testing may result in sanctions, including entry of an order dismissing the paternity action without prejudice.

● The conference officer shall advise and provide written notice to the parties that they may enter into a written stipulation whereby both agree to submit to genetic testing for the purpose of resolving finally the issue of paternity. If the test results indicate a 99% or higher probability of paternity, the defendant shall be stipulated to be the biological father of the child and the case referred for a child support conference. If the test results indicate an exclusion, the action shall be dismissed. The written stipulation constitutes a waiver of the right to a hearing on the genetic testing or trial on the issue of paternity.

● The conference officer shall advise and provide written notice to the parties that if they do not enter into a written stipulation and the test results do not indicate an exclusion, there will be a hearing regarding genetic testing or trial before a judge without a jury on the issue of paternity in accordance with the procedures set forth in subdivision (d) of this rule.

POST-TESTING PROCEDURES

The results of the genetic tests shall be provided in writing to counsel for the parties or, if unrepresented, to the parties themselves.

If the results of the genetic tests resolve the issue of paternity pursuant to the stipulation of the parties, a paternity order shall be entered and served on the parties. If the defendant is excluded, the action shall be dismissed. If the defendant is stipulated to be the biological father, the action shall proceed as in other actions for support.

If the results of the genetic tests do not resolve the issue of paternity pursuant to the stipulation of the parties, but the test results indicate a 99% or more probability of paternity, the court shall issue a rule against the defendant to show cause why an order should not be entered finding him to be the father. The rule shall advise the defendant that pursuant to 23 Pa.C.S. § 4343 his defense is limited to a showing by clear and convincing evidence that the results of the genetic tests are not reliable. The rule shall direct that an answer be filed within twenty days after service of the rule on the defendant. The answer shall state the material facts which constitute this defense. Any allegation of fact which does not appear of record must be verified.

If an answer is not timely filed, the court shall enter an order finding paternity and refer the action to conference and hearing as in other actions for support. If an answer is filed raising a disputed issue of material fact relating to the reliability of the genetic testing, the case shall be listed promptly for expedited hearing before a judge. The burden of proof at the hearing is on the defendant and is limited to proof by clear and convincing evidence that the results of the genetic tests are not reliable.

If the results of the genetic tests do not resolve the issue of paternity and the test results indicate less than a 99% probability of paternity, the case shall be promptly listed for expedited trial before a judge.

If, after a hearing or trial, the decision is for the defendant on the issue of paternity, a final order shall be entered by the court dismissing the action as to the child. If the decision is against the defendant on the issue of paternity, an *interlocutory order* shall be entered by the court finding paternity. An Interlocutory Order is an order that is not final. Generally, it is an order that serves as an interim directive pending finalization of certain aspects of a case.

The court may enter an interim order for child support at that time and shall refer the action to conference and hearing as in other actions for support.

If defendant fails to appear as ordered for a conference, hearing or trial, or for genetic tests, the court shall, upon proof of service on the defendant, enter an order establishing paternity. The court may also enter an interim order for child support at that time and shall refer the action to conference and hearing as in other actions for support.

An order establishing paternity is not an appealable order. The issue of paternity may be included in an appeal from the final order of child support.

Section 3: Visitation

VISITATION 8
OVERVIEW AND
AGREEMENT

Visitation is a term which is *infrequently used* in the Commonwealth of Pennsylvania as it is uncommon and undesirable to limit a child's time with a parent to simply "visiting". Generally some negative issues or parental mis-deeds have resulted in such limitation of parental time.

Visitation is the part of the court order that defines the conditions for the non-custodial parent to have contact with the child. Visitation is limited by legal custody being vested in the other parent. This means that visitation does not give one the authority to conflict with the long-range decisions and policies of the parent with legal custody. For instance, if the parent with legal custody has decided to raise the child in the Catholic faith, the parent with visitation rights may not take the child to be entered into the Hindu tradition.

SUPERVISED VISITATION

There are no reported cases of a court honoring complete denial of visitation for a parent. Even in cases of abuse, courts have upheld supervised visitation. Supervised visitation occurs when the parent is allowed to visit with the child only while in the company of another person. This person usually is a friend or a relative whom the two parents agree will be allowed to act as a chaperon. Supervised visitation often calls for a restriction of visitation to a particular location and time.

THOSE WHO GET VISITATION

Who can be awarded visitation? Obviously, a biological parent can be awarded visitation. Additionally, grandparents (even when the parents were not married or are not currently divorced) and step-parents may be awarded visitation rights.

When can visitation be denied? The court has the power to deny visitation. Normally the court will only stop visitation for a certain time or until a certain task is performed. For example, the court has previously withheld visitation until the parent met their financial obligation. If your spouse should deny you court ordered visitation, you first file for a modification of visitation for a more definite schedule, before filing a contempt action. Many parents feel they have the right to stop paying child support when denied visitation, but they are very incorrect! Withholding of child support will only get a parent into serious trouble and possibly may get the parent arrested.

VISITATION AGREEMENT

The court will regularly abide by and ratify any custody and visitation arrangement you and your spouse can agree upon, as long as your agreement does not present itself to the judge as one that is detrimental to the child or children. Most of this section will discuss the way in which custody and visitation decisions will be made when you and your spouse cannot reach an agreement.

When there is a minor child or children, you and your spouse will need to go through the court's custody office. The mission of the custody office is a multiple one:

- to assist you in formalizing your custody agreement, if you have one;

- to attempt to assist you in reaching an agreement; and,

- to make a recommendation to the judge about custody and visitation if no agreement can be reached.

The following inquiries and responses will guide you through the custody process:

Inquiry: Are you and your spouse in agreement with respect to the shared custody of your child (children)?

YES: 1. Call the custody office for an appointment.

2. Attend an intake conference (this is the first meeting with the custody officer).

3. Attend the "Children Coping With Divorce" seminar. This is an informative and required, seminar addressing the needs and concerns of children who are caught in the divorce process.

NO: 1. File a petition.

2. Attend the "Children Coping With Divorce" seminar.

3. Attend an intake conference.

Inquiry: Did an agreement result from the Custody Intake Conference?

YES: No further action is necessary. You will receive a copy of the handwritten agreement at the end of the intake conference. In a week to ten days, you will receive your Court Order.

NO: A temporary order will be issued and a Custody Conference will be scheduled.

Inquiry: Did the Custody conference result in a custody agreement?

    YES: Further action is not necessary. You will receive a copy of the handwritten agreement at the end of the Custody Conference. In a week to ten days, you will receive your Court Order.

    NO: The Conciliator will prepare a Recommended Order and forward it to the Court. You must follow this order unless it is changed by another Court Order.

Inquiry: Do you agree with the Recommended Order?

    YES: No further action is necessary. In a week to ten days, you will receive the Court Order.

    NO: If you object to the Recommended Order, you may file a Request for Adversarial Hearing within ten days from the date you receive the Recommended Order in the mail. You may telephone the custody office to obtain a Request for Adversarial Hearing form. Each county has its own requirements. There is a fee, usually about $50, to request an adversarial hearing. The adversarial hearing will be before a judge.

DENIED VISITATION

If the custodial parent is denying you access to your child for visitation, you may seek a court order defining your visitation rights. Violation of this court order will result in the custodial parent being held in contempt of court.

SECTION 4:
CHILD SUPPORT

CHILD SUPPORT OVERVIEW 9

An unfortunate fact of economic life is that a family cannot live as cheaply divided as it can together. Thus, after a divorce, the living standard of the entire family is often lowered and the court often finds itself in the unenviable position of having to divide a scarcity of resources. Then too, there is the problem of changing the child support order to meet changing needs of children and enforcing court orders against fathers and mothers who either refuse to make court ordered child support payments or who cannot do so due to circumstances beyond their control. These problems, when added to the issue of custody, visitation and the division of property in a divorce, keep the family law courts of the country packed to capacity.

Both parents have a legal duty to support their child according to their ability to do so. Since 1990, Pennsylvania has had child support guidelines in effect, which provide a formula for calculating child support based on a proportion of each parent's gross income. These guidelines are applied unless a party can show that application of the guidelines would be unjust and inappropriate in a particular case.

This section discusses the issue of child support when viewed in the context of a divorce or paternity action. Just as courts must often make the crucial decision as to child custody and visitation, so too must it often determine how much child support the non-custodial parent will be ordered to pay. This section will describe the considerations that a court will take into account when deciding the issue of child support, whether in a divorce or a paternity case. It will also describe the methods by which child support orders are enforced by courts and how to modify an order for support.

Establishing Child Support Payments

During a marriage or committed relationship, such issues are rarely a concern for the court. But when parents divorce or cease to live together with their children as a family, the courts are usually required to establish by decree the amount of child support a non-custodial parent must pay. Like the issue of custody, this can be reached by agreement or by fighting it out in front of a judge. Child support payments, like alimony, may be incorporated into the divorce judgment or may be provided for in a marital separation agreement. You can avoid making child support a contested issue, and the legal expense of litigating this issue before a *Master* or a judge by both parents agreeing to the appropriate amount of child support and making this agreement part of a marital separation agreement. (A *Master* is a court appointed authority who determines the distribution of the parties' assets in a divorce case.)

The Nature of the Child Support Order

There are several parts to most child support orders. First and foremost, the paying parent will be ordered to make a monthly money payment to the custodial parent. The order will typically read, in part, as follows:

> Father (name) is directed and ordered to pay directly to mother (name) as and for child support of two (2) children namely Robert and Cindy, the sum of $325 per month, per child for a total of $650, payable on the first day of each month, said payments to continue until each such child shall die, reach majority, become emancipated or until further order of court.

Pay Directly to the Parent

Many paying parents resent the child support order because it is made directly to the custodial parent and not the children. Because of this, some refuse to make the payments because they see it as a form of alimony. However, this is not true. The direct payments are to be used to pay for the vital needs of the children, such as rent, food, and clothes.

NOTE: *Visitation rights may not be denied to the non-custodial parent, even though the non-custodial parent is not paying child support.*

Changing the Order

A child support order is not set in concrete but is subject to change should future conditions warrant. Thus, either parent may petition the court to raise or lower support should conditions warrant.

Ending Payments

The purpose of this language is to provide for an automatic end to the support obligation when the child reaches eighteen (18) years old or dies. However, the issue of emancipation is often in dispute and may require a court determination. Courts may order the parent paying child support to continue making payments if the child enters college, but will generally not do this if it will impose a hardship on the parents.

CALCULATING AND DETERMINING CHILD SUPPORT 10

Courts in Pennsylvania follow the statutory child support guidelines, commonly know as the *Grid*. The court will not let you bargain away your child's right to child support. Generally, child support payments are for the ordinary expenses of food, shelter, clothing, education and medication needs for the children only.

FACTORS FOR THE COURT

In determining an award of child support, a court will look at all relevant facts upon the following issues:

The Needs of the Children. A sickly or developmentally disabled child will often require a higher level of support than a healthy child.

The Age of the Children. Infants and younger children often cost less to support than older children.

The Ability of the Non-custodial Parent to Pay. The court is limited in awarding child support by the ability of a parent to pay based on income from all sources, often including a new spouse's earnings.

The Earning Capacity of the Custodial Parent. Both parents have the duty to support their children, not just the paying parent. Thus, the earnings or earning capacity of the custodial parent which are available to provide support for the children, and perhaps that of their new spouse, will also be considered when determining child support levels.

OTHER RESPONSIBILITIES OF THE PARENTS

The other lawful responsibilities of both parents will also be looked into in determining child support. For example, if the non-custodial parent is paying child support from a previous marriage (a rather common occurrence), the court will take that obligation into consideration. Necessities of life, such as rent and food will also be taken into account by the court. However, the court will not reduce child support payments to make it easier for the parent to pay discretionary obligations. For example, a parent cannot provide for a charity or buy an expensive car at the expense of providing for his or her own children.

To assist the court in determining the proper amount of support, both parties will be required by the court to prepare a financial declaration that is signed under penalty of perjury. Each parent will be required to disclose fully all income derived form all source including those monies earned by a new spouse or a live-in-lover. Further, the nature and extent of the parents' property holdings such as bank accounts, investments, real property, and their financial obligations are fully within the scope of review for the court. The court will rely heavily on these documents in making the order and thus it is in the best interests of the children that the declarations be filled out completely and honestly.

SUPPORT HEARINGS

Child support hearings are often *adversarial*. That means that when the parents cannot agree on the support order, (sometimes after mediation), the court, through a Master's hearing, will hold a hearing to decide the issue. (This is sometimes done in a chambers conference to save time.) At the hearing, each spouse (or their lawyer) will have the opportunity to cross examine the other on issues relevant to the support issue and each can subpoena documents and call witnesses to support his or her position as to the amount of child support that should be paid. Child support orders can also be appealed, although the likelihood of success is very slim.

The reason for the implementation of the guidelines is that the Pennsylvania Legislature has decided that a parent has a legal obligation to provide support for the child [in proportion to his or her gross earnings].

ISSUES EFFECTING SUPPORT OBLIGATIONS

Several issues effect the payment of child support. Some of these issues will also allow a change in a support order after the order is made.

DIVIDED OR
SPLIT CUSTODY
OF MINOR
CHILDREN

Where one or more children reside with each party, the guidelines for "spouse and children" will be used instead of the guidelines for children only, provided that the parties are still married or, if the parties are divorced, there is an agreement or an order for alimony or an order for unallocated spousal and child support. In cases where there is no obligation for spousal support, the guidelines for children only will apply.

Example 1. If the parties are married with two children, one of whom resides with each spouse, and the net monthly incomes of the husband and wife are $1,500 and $800 respectively, the guideline amount is computed from the grid as follows. Using the grid for "Spouse and 1 Child", the husband's obligation to the wife is $405. Using the same grid, the wife's obligation to the husband is $148. Subtracting $148 from $405 produces a guideline amount of $251 for the husband's payment to the wife. The husband will have a total income of $1,243 per month to support himself and the child residing with him. The wife will have $1,057 per month for herself and the child residing with her.

Example 2. As in Example 1, the parties are married with two children, one of whom resides with each spouse. However, the husband's net monthly income is $4,000, the formula must be used to determine the wife's obligation to the husband, i.e., $162. Subtracting the wife's obligation from the husband's obligation results in a guideline payment from the husband to the wife of $1,056.

The procedure should not necessarily be followed where one party's income is minimal and the other party's income is significantly greater.

Example: The non-custodial parent's income is $2,000 and custodial parent has no income, the guideline for one child is $390 because the parent without income is not liable for support which would reduce the $390 order. This result is inequitable, and therefore the formula set forth above should not be used in similar situations.

CHILD CARE EXPENSES	Reasonable child care expenses paid by the custodial parent, if necessary to maintain employment or appropriate education in pursuit of income, are the responsibility of both parents. Normally, the burden will be divided equally between the parents by determining the reasonable child care expenses and adding one-half of this amount to the obligor's monthly obligation.
POST-SECONDARY EDUCATIONAL EXPENSES.	Determination of educational expenses for adult children enrolled in a post-high school program is governed by the applicable law(23 Pa.Conn.Stat., Tit. 23, beginning with Sec. 4327.)
PRIVATE SCHOOL TUITION, SUMMER CAMP, AND OTHER NEEDS	The support grids do not take into consideration expenditures for private school tuition, summer camp or other needs of a child which are not specifically addressed by the guidelines. If the *trier-of-fact* (judge or jury) determines that one or more such needs are reasonable, the expense thereof shall be borne by the parties in reasonable shares. The *obligor's* (the one who has to pay) reasonable share may be added to the monthly support obligation.
DIRECT CONTRIBUTIONS OF NON-CUSTODIAL PARENT	The support guidelines contemplate that the non-custodial parent has regular contact, including vacation time, with his or her children, and that he or she makes direct expenditures on behalf of the children. Thus, a non-custodial parent's support obligation should be reduced only if that parent spends an unusual amount of time with the children.
SUPPORT WITH MULTIPLE FAMILIES	The goal of the guidelines is to treat each child equitably. Where the total of obligor's support obligations equals fifty percent or less of net income, there will generally be no deviation from the guideline amount of support on the ground of the existence of a new family. If the total of obligor's support obligations exceeds fifty percent, the trier-of-fact may consider a reduction.

CHILD SUPPORT CALCULATION

In Pennsylvania, as in most states, the question of child support is mostly a matter of a mathematical calculation. Getting a fair child support amount depends upon the accuracy of the income information presented to the court. If you feel fairly sure that the information your spouse presents is accurate, or that you have obtained accurate information about his or her income, there is not much to debate. The court will simply take the income information provided, use the formula to calculate the amount, and order that amount to be paid.

In most cases, there will not be much room to argue about the amount of child support, so there usually is not a need to get an attorney. If you claim your spouse has not provided accurate income information, this may be the time to consult an attorney, who will know how to obtain more accurate income information. Your attorney (or you) may set up a support conference before a support counselor at your county courthouse. A support counselor reviews your income along with your spouse's income to determine the amount of support.

If child support is involved in your case, you should first work out what you think the court will order based upon the child support guidelines discussed on page 203. Do this before discussing the matter with your spouse. The parent who possesses the bulk of the custody time with the child(ren) will be entitled to an award of child support. If you will be receiving child support, you may want to ask for more than the guidelines require, and negotiate down to what the guidelines suggest. If you will be paying child support, you may want to try for slightly less than the guidelines call for, but keep in mind that the support counselor will probably look at the schedule and ask questions if you and your spouse are agreeing to less. This does not mean the support counselor will reject your agreement, but you may need to offer an explanation as to why you are not following the guidelines. You can tell your spouse that there is little room for negotiation on child support as the court will probably require it be set according to the statute. If your spouse will not agree on something very close to the guidelines, give up trying to work it out and let the support counselor decide.

Pennsylvania law establishes the legal duty to provide financial support for children and spouses. Once again, the master will probably agree with any arrangement you and your spouse reach, as long as he or she is satisfied that the child will be taken care of adequately. The following information and the Domestic Relations INCOME AND EXPENSE STATEMENT will give you an idea of your financial base regarding child support. (see form 2, page 201).

NOTE: *You may also hear attorneys, judges, and other court personnel refer to form 2 as a Child Support Income and Expense Questionnaire or a Financial Affidavit.*

Make a copy of the SUPPORT GUIDELINE COMPUTATIONS—CHILD SUPPORT to use as a worksheet to get a rough idea of your income and expenses. (see form 3, p.203). Later, as you prepare to file, you will refer back to this section for instructions on completing the form.

Where an agreement cannot be reached, the following procedure will be used. Generally, there are two factors used to determine the amount of support to be paid:

- the needs of the child; and

- the financial ability of each parent to meet those needs.

Pennsylvania has simplified this procedure by establishing a formula to be used in calculating both the needs of the child and each parent's ability to meet those needs. In filling out the SUPPORT GUIDELINE COMPUTATIONS—CHILD SUPPORT, be sure to convert everything to monthly amounts. (see form 3, p.203). The following steps are used in determining the proper amount of support:

STEP 1. Determine each party's average monthly gross income. This is usually done by taking the gross income for the past six months and dividing by six. Gross income includes:

- wages, salary, fees, and commissions;

- net income from business or dealings in property, interest, rents, royalties, and dividends, pensions and all forms of retirement;

- income from an interest in an estate or trust,

- alimony paid to you;

- social security benefits, temporary and permanent disability benefits, workmen's compensation, and unemployment compensation;

- capability of income is considered when a party willfully fails to obtain appropriate employment (age, education, work experience, etc., are considered in determining earning capacity);

- bonuses, may be annualized and considered carefully, particularly in times of economic difficulty; or,

- income from seasonal employment, which will ordinarily be based upon a yearly average.

STEP 2. Determine each party's net income. Net income is determined by taking the gross income, and subtracting the following items:

- federal, state, and local income taxes, FICA payments;

- non-voluntary retirement payments, and union dues;

- health insurance premiums for the benefit of the other party or the child(ren); and,

- alimony paid to the other party.

STEP 3. Apply the child support guidelines. The example of form 3 on page 194 is based upon support of a wife and one minor child. The defendant earns $1,053 per month net (i.e., after allowed deductions are subtracted from gross income). The plaintiff earns $725 per month net. Find the appropriate percentage on the Chart of Proportional Expenditures on page 195, and follow the self-explanatory mathematical formula on form 3. For one minor child, with combined incomes of $1,778, the percentage is twenty percent (which will be .20 in the mathematical calculation). The defendant's obligation would be $209.80 per month for one child, and $35.46 per month for spousal support, for a total of $246.26 per month for a wife and one minor child.

NOTE: *The chart on page 195 is the chart in effect at the time this book went to press. Since this chart can change at any time, you should obtain the most current chart from the prothonotary, the Court's Support office, or a law library.*

STEP 4. Determine if there are special circumstances that justify a further adjustment. In deciding whether or not to use the amount of support determined by the guidelines, the judge will consider:

- unusual needs and unusual fixed obligations;
- other support obligations of the parties;
- other income in the household;
- ages of the children;
- assets of the parties;
- medical expenses not covered by insurance;
- standard of living of the parties and their children; and,
- other relevant and appropriate 'factors, including the best interests of the child.

NOTE: *Failure to deviate from the guidelines by considering a party's actual expenditures where there are special needs and special circumstances is a misapplication of the guidelines.*

The deviation applies to the amount of the support obligation, not to the amount of income. The court may apply a ten percent deviation up or down depending upon certain circumstances.

CHILD SUPPORT ENFORCEMENT 11

A child support order is as enforceable as any other court judgment or decree. Thus, a parent who is not paid child support can use each and every legal tool available to enforce the order, including:

- wage garnishments,

- wage assignments,

- contempt of court decrees; and,

- seizure of the non-payor's property by writ of execution.

The child support decree is not limited to an order of direct money payments to the custodial parent. Other areas of providing for the children's needs are also usually addressed. The following language is an example of a typical child support order:

As and for additional child support, father (name) is ordered to maintain his children as beneficiaries on his health and life insurance policies available through his employment. Father is further ordered to pay for one-half of all uninsured medical, dental and ophthalmologic services provided for the children

> As and for additional child support, father shall pay directly to the X's Daycare Center, the full cost of afternoon after-school day care. However, should the children be enrolled in morning day care, or should maternal grandmother care for the children, such expenses shall be the sole responsibility of the mother.

> As and for additional child support, father shall pay the round-trip plane and other reasonable costs of transporting the children for visitation with father, as provided in the visitation provisions of this order.

These clauses illustrate the fluid and flexible nature of child support orders and the wide latitude a court has in creating a support arrangement it deems in the best interests of the children. (The court will try to maintain the lifestyle the children enjoyed before the divorce if the parents' finances permit.) Thus, a parent can be ordered to maintain insurance for the benefit of children, pay medical bills, private school expenses, day care costs, transportation bills, music lessons and to pay or partially pay for other aspects of a child's day-to-day life, activities and upbringing. The amount of support can also be reduced should the non-custodial parent have physical custody of the children for at least 35% of the time.

CHILD SUPPORT AGENCIES

There are two agencies you need to be familiar with:

CENTRAL
COLLECTION
OFFICE

The *collections office* is the agency that processes the child support (and alimony) payments. A Support Collections Office is located within the courthouse in your locale, although a main processing center is based in the state capitol in Harrisburg, Pennsylvania. All processing of support orders are now computerized, and the main data bank records the transactions on each individual case. You local collections office can assist you with any problems you may experience in collecting or paying support. The monies for support are paid by the support payer or obligor directly to the support payee or recipient as mandated from the main office and enforced and monitored through the local office. This is frequently a division of the support office. The spouse responsible to pay the support (or his or her employer) will make payments to the depository. The collection's office then cashes that check and issues a check to the spouse entitled to receive support.

CHILD SUPPORT ENFORCEMENT OFFICE

The Child Support Enforcement Office is responsible for enforcing the payment of child support to parents receiving support, and others who request their services. If you are to receive support and you would like to use the enforcement services of this office, you will need to contact your local child support enforcement office. This may not be necessary if your spouse goes on an income deduction order immediately, and keeps his or her job. But if some payments are missed, you may call the Child Support Enforcement Office at any time and ask for their assistance. Income deductions are monies withheld and withdrawn directly from the support obligor's paycheck. Thus, the support monies are paid directly from the Central Processing Office to the support recipient. Be aware, that because of the extended nature of the bureaucracy involved in processing the support deductions, it is likely that payments run behind and routinely are not timely.

NOTE: *Income deduction is mandatory in Pennsylvania.*

Enforcement Agencies -
Bureau of Child Support Enforcement
Department of Public Welfare, PO Box 8018
Harrisburg, PA 17105
717-787-3672
800-932-0211

SECTION 5: PROCEDURES AND MODIFICATIONS

AN INTRODUCTION TO LEGAL FORMS 12

NOTE: *It is best to make photocopies of the forms, and keep the originals blank to use in case you make mistakes, or need additional copies.*

Most of the forms in Appendix G of this book follow forms created and officially approved by either the Pennsylvania Supreme Court or by the Philadelphia County Family Court. These forms have one advantage- the prothonotary and judges are not likely to object to them. The forms in this book are legally correct, however, one occasionally encounters a troublesome prothonotary or judge who is very particular about how he or she wants the forms drafted. If you encounter any problem with the forms in this book being accepted by the prothonotary or judge, you can try one or more of the following:

- ask the prothonotary or judge what is wrong with your form, then try to change it to suit the prothonotary or judge. Many counties have their own versions or peculiarities to standard formats, or

- ask the prothonotary or judge if there is a Pennsylvania Supreme Court form (or a county-specific form) available. If there is, find out where you can get it, then get it and use it. The instructions in this book will still help you to fill it out.

NOTE: *If you will be filing your custody, visitation, or support matters in Philadelphia County, you will find the court is very particular about how things must be done, and has its own required forms. In Appendix G, you will find some forms that are required in Philadelphia County. You may find that you need to obtain the forms directly from the Philadelphia Family Court Clerk's Office.*

NOTE: *Although the instructions in this book will tell you to "type in" certain information, it is not absolutely necessary to use a typewriter. If typing is not possible, you can print the information required in the forms, as long as it can easily be read, or the Prothonotary's office may not accept your papers for filing.*

> *Warning:* Some, if not all, of the counties require the use of *black ink*. If you write in the information instead of typing, be sure to use a pen with *black ink*. However, when you sign any form, use *blue ink*. Never use red, green, or any other unusual ink color.

Each form is referred to by both the title of the form and a form number. Be sure to check the form name and number because some of the forms have similar sounding names. Also, a list of the forms, by name, is found at the beginning of Appendix G. You will notice that most of the forms in Appendix G have the similar headings which identify the court, the parties, and the case number.

The top portion of these court forms will all be completed as follows:

- ☛ Fill in the name of the county in which you will file your papers.

- ☛ Fill in the case number. There may also be a division designation that is to indicate which judge is assigned to your case number and division will be assigned when you file your and any other initial papers with the prothonotary. The prothonotary will write in the case number and division on your Petition for Custody and any other initial papers with the prothonotary. The prothonotary will write in the case number and division on your paper. You will fill in the same number and division on any papers you file at a later date.

☞ Fill in your full name on the line marked "Petitioner" or "Plaintiff" and your spouse's full name on the line marked "Respondent" or "Defendant." Do not use nicknames or shortened versions of names. You should use the names as they appear on your marriage license, or divorce papers, if possible.

When completed, the top portion of your forms should look something like the following example:

COURT OF COMMON PLEAS OF ERIE COUNTY, PENNSYLVANIA

Juliet Capulet,

Plaintiff   Case Number 14251-2001

v.   Division: FAMILY

Romeo Montague,

Defendant

At the end of many of the forms there will be a place for you to sign your name, and type in your name, address, and phone number. You will also notice that your signature must be notarized on certain forms, in which case a provision is included on the form for completion by the *notary public*. A notary public is a person authorized by the Commonwealth of Pennsylvania to administer oaths, take affidavits, certify documents, and to validate signatures of an individual who is present to so sign or to so state.

FILING WITH THE PROTHONOTARY

Once you decide which forms you need, and have them all prepared, it is time to file your case with the prothonotary. First, make at least five copies of each form (the original for the Prothonotary, one copy for the Custody Office, one for yourself, one for your spouse, and one extra just in case the prothonotary asks for two copies or you decide to hire an attorney later).

Filing is a simple process, but the following information will help things go even more smoothly. Call the prothonotary's office. You can find the phone number under the county government section of your phone directory. Ask the following questions (along with any other questions that come to mind, such as where the prothonotary's office is located and what are there hours);

- How much is the filing fee for a Petition for Custody?

- Does the court have any special forms that need to be filed with the Petition for Custody? (If there are special forms that do not appear in this book, you will need to go to the prothonotary's office and pick them up. There may be a fee; so ask.)

- How many copies of the Petition and other forms do you need to file with the Prothonotary?

Next, take your PETITION FOR (TEMPORARY) CUSTODY (form 6, p.209), and any other forms you determine you need, to the Custody Office. Then, once that form is *processed in* (into the system and stamped) while you wait, you will take it to the prothonotary's office to file and be assigned a docket number. (Instructions for completing these forms are provided in other parts of this book.) The prothonotary handles many different types of cases, so be sure to look for signs telling you which office or window to go to. You should be looking for signs that say such things as "Family Court;' "Family Division," "Filing," etc. If it is too confusing, ask someone where to file a Petition for Custody.

Once you have found the right place, simply hand the papers to the prothonotary and say, "I'd like to file this." The prothonotary will examine the papers, then do one of two things: either accept it for filing (and either collect the filing fee or direct you to where to pay it), or tell you that something is not correct. If you are told something is wrong, ask the prothonotary to explain to you what is wrong and how to correct the problem. Although prothonotaries are not permitted to give legal advice, the types of problems they spot are usually very minor things that they can tell you how to correct. Often it is possible to figure out how to correct it from the way they explain what is wrong.

Notifying Your Spouse, Mate, Etc.

A basic sense of fairness (in addition to the laws of Pennsylvania) requires that a person be notified of a legal proceeding that involves him or her. In all cases, you are required to notify your spouse that you have filed for custody, visitation, and support. This gives your spouse a chance to respond to your Petition(s). If you are unable to find your spouse (and therefore cannot have him or her served by certified mail-return receipt requested) you may choose to have him or her personally served by the Sheriff or Constable. "Service" upon a party is made by delivering the document(s) to that individual either by a specified form of mail or by delivery by a person of suitable age (18 years or older and mentally competent).

"Certified mail—return receipt requested" is a mailing process which can be requested at your local post office for a small fee. The certified mail process ensures that the designated recipient will receive your documentation in that such party must sign for the parcel. Once the party has received and signed for the parcel a green card is returned to you indicating that your party has been "served." If your spouse cannot be found, see the subsection entitled "If You Can't Find Your Spouse." The notice requirements as they relate to your particular situation, will be discussed in later chapters.

Notice of Filing the Complaint

The usual way to notify your spouse that you filed for custody, visitation, or support is called *certified service*, which is done by mail. Certified service involves mailing your documents by "certified mail, return receipt requested." A green card is attached to the envelope containing copies of your Petition. Your spouse will have to sign this card in order to get the envelope from the mailman or post office. The signed card is then returned to you, which will appropriately document your mailing and your spouse's receipt of the papers. There is a minimal fee for this service (usually about $3 to $4 in addition to the postage stamp).

NOTE: *Process serving by mail (Certified mail—return receipt requested) information can be found on the USPS website at:*
http://www.usps.com

Other Notices

Once your spouse has been served with the Petition for Custody, you may simply mail him or her copies of any papers you file later. All you need to do is sign a statement called a CERTIFICATE OF SERVICE verifying that you mailed copies to your spouse. Some of the forms in this book will include a CERTIFICATE OF SERVICE section for you to complete. If any form you file does not contain one, you will need to complete the CERTIFICATE OF SERVICE (see form 4, p.205.) The form is rather clear about what information is to be entered by you. On the line after the phrase: "I Certify That The," type in the title of what you are sending, such as "Petition for Temporary Custody." Form 4 is to be filed with the prothonotary as proof that you sent a copy to you spouse.

SETTING A HEARING

If you should set a hearing date for any child or spousal support, or child custody matters, you will need to notify your spouse. Setting the date for a support hearing simply requires that you go to the Support office and request a hearing date and time. The support officer will have you complete certain paperwork, and you will later receive a notice of the date and time of the hearing. Once you know your hearing date and time, you must send a notice to your spouse. This is done by preparing a NOTICE OF HEARING (see form 8, p.215.)

☛ Fill in the top of the form according to the instructions on pages 78–79.

☛ Type in your spouse's name and address (or his or her attorney's name and address) on the lines after the word "TO."

☛ Fill in all of the blanks on the form for the court or judge's name, date, time, and location of the hearing (including the name and address of the courthouse).

☛ On the line after the phrase "on the following matter" type in the kind of hearing, such as "Motion for Support or Custody."

☛ Make three copies of the Notice of Hearing, and mail one copy to your spouse. File the original with the custody office and keep two copies for yourself.

COURTROOM MANNERS

There are certain rules of procedure that are used in a court. These are essentially rules of good conduct, or good manners, and are designed to keep the proceedings orderly. Many of the rules are written down, although some are unwritten customs that have developed over many years. They are not difficult, and most of them make sense. Following these suggestions will make the judge respect you for your maturity and professional manner, and possibly even make him or her forget for a moment that you are not a lawyer. It will also increase the likelihood that you will receive the things you request.

SHOWING RESPECT FOR THE JUDGE

Showing respect basically means do not do anything to make the judge angry with you, such as arguing with him or her. Be polite, and, call the judge "Your Honor" when you speak to him or her, such as "Yes, Your Honor," or "Your Honor, I brought proof of my income." Although many lawyers address judges as "Judge," this is not proper. You should wear appropriate clothing (coat and tie for men and a dress or suit for women). Do not wear T-shirts, blue jeans, shorts, or "revealing" clothing. Many of the following rules also relate to showing respect for the court.

WHEN THE JUDGE TALKS, YOU LISTEN

Anytime the judge is talking, you need to be listening carefully. Even if the judge interrupts you, stop talking immediately and listen. Judges can become upset if you do not allow them to interrupt.

ONLY ONE PERSON CAN TALK AT A TIME

Each person is allotted his or her own time to talk in court. The judge can only listen to one person at a time, so do not interrupt your spouse when it is his or her turn. As difficult as it may be, stop talking if your spouse interrupts you. (Let the judge tell your spouse to keep quiet and let you have your say.)

TALK TO THE JUDGE, NOT TO YOUR SPOUSE

Many couples come before a judge and begin arguing with each other. They turn away from the judge, face each other, and begin arguing as if they were in a room alone. Usually, this has several negative results: The judge cannot understand what either one is saying since they both start talking at once, they both look like fools for losing control, and the judge becomes angry with both of them. Whenever you speak in a courtroom, look only at the judge. Try to pretend that your spouse is not there. Remember, you are there to convince the judge that you should have the children, the visits, the support, and so on. You do not need to convince your spouse.

TALK ONLY WHEN IT IS YOUR TURN

The usual procedure is for you to present your case first. When you have completed saying all you came to say, your spouse will have a chance to say whatever he or she came to say. Let your spouse have his or her say. When he or she is finished, you will have another chance to respond to what has been said.

STICK TO THE SUBJECT	Many people tend to get off the track and start telling the judge all the problems with their marriage over the past twenty years. This wastes time and aggravates the judge. Stick to the subject, and answer the judge's questions simply and to the point.
KEEP CALM	Judges like matters to go smoothly in their courtrooms. They do not like shouting, name calling, crying, or other displays of emotion. Generally, judges do not like family law cases because they get too emotionally charged. So, give your judge a pleasant surprise by keeping calm and focus on the issues.
SHOW RESPECT FOR YOUR SPOUSE	Even if you do not respect your spouse, act as though you do. All you have to do is refer to your spouse as "Mr. Smith" or "Ms. Smith" (using his or her correct name, of course).

SPECIAL CIRCUMSTANCES 13

This section will address certain "special circumstances," or particular situations that may arise in your case. These are circumstances that may not arise in *all* cases, however they do manifest themselves in a number of Domestic Relations matters. Therefore, it is helpful to have these issues briefly highlighted in the event that such conditions should arise in your case.

WHEN YOU CANNOT AFFORD COURT COSTS

If you cannot afford to pay court costs, such as filing fees and sheriff service fees, you should go to the prothonotary office, which is usually located at your county courthouse. Tell the prothonotary that you wish to file for a domestic relations claim, but are unable to afford the filing fee and other court costs. The prothonotary will verify your financial status to determine if you qualify, and provide you with the necessary information and forms to have the court costs either waived or reduced.

If you are involved in a custody case and are experiencing financial hardship, your local legal aid office will often appoint an attorney (at no charge to you) to handle your custody case. These are volunteer lawyers who offer their time and service to handle such cases.

PROTECTING YOURSELF AND YOUR CHILDREN

Some people have special concerns when getting prepared to file for a divorce:

- fear of physical attack by their spouse;

- fear that their spouse will try to take the marital property and hide it; and,

- tender or very young age of child(ren) or special educational needs of child(ren).

Battering is the single greatest cause of injury to women-more than rapes, muggings, and auto accidents combined. Four million American women are battered each year, and every fifteen seconds a woman in the United States is beaten by her husband, ex-husband, or boyfriend. At the time of this writing, it is estimated that four thousand women die each year because of domestic violence.

PROTECTING YOUR CHILDREN

If you are worried that your spouse may try to kidnap your children, you should make sure that the day care center, baby-sitter, relative, or whomever you leave the children with at any time, is aware that you are in the process of a divorce and that the children are only to be released to you personally (not to your spouse or to any other relative, friend, etc.). To prevent your spouse from taking the children out of the United States, you can apply for a passport for each child. Once a passport is issued, the government will not issue another. Lock the passport up in a safe deposit box. (This will not prevent them from being taken to Canada or Mexico, where passports are not required, but will prevent them from being taken overseas.) You can also prepare a motion to prevent the removal of the children from the state and to deny passport services. Also, the State Department usually requires both parents to, sign for passport processing and documentation for their children. You may obtain forms for this motion from the prothonotary or your local law library.

If your spouse is determined and resourceful, there is no guaranteed way to prevent the concerns discussed in this chapter from happening. All you can do is put as many obstacles in his or her way as possible, and prepare for him or her to suffer legal consequences (e.g., fine or jail) for acting improperly.

TEMPORARY SUPPORT AND CUSTODY

If your spouse has left you with the children, the mortgage and monthly bills, and is not helping you financially, you may want to ask the court to order the payment of support for you and the children during the divorce procedure. Of course, if you were the only person bringing in income and have been paying all the bills, do not expect to get any temporary support. To request temporary support, go to the support office in your county. The personnel at the support office will assist you in seeking temporary support.

To seek a temporary child custody order, you will need to go to the support or custody office for your county and request a hearing for support or custody. To complete the PETITION FOR (TEMPORARY) CUSTODY (see form 6, p.209):

- ☛ Complete the top portion of the form according to the instructions in Chapter 12.
- ☛ Type your name on the line in the first, unnumbered paragraph.
- ☛ In paragraph I, type your name on the first line, and your street address, city, and zip code on the other lines.
- ☛ In paragraph 2, type in your spouse's name and address on the appropriate lines.

☞ In paragraph 3, fill in the date you were married, and the date you and your spouse separated.

☞ In paragraph 4, fill in the date of birth for each child.

☞ In paragraph 5, indicate who your children are currently living with. Type in the word "Petitioner" if the children are in your physical custody, or the "Respondent" if they are in the physical custody of your spouse. If the children are living with someone other than you or your spouse (such as a grandparent, aunt, or friend), fill in the name of the person they are living with, and that person's relationship to you.

☞ In paragraph 6, list any medical conditions of any of the children. If there are no special significant medical conditions, type in "none."

☞ In paragraph 7, indicate the number of years during which the children have resided with you. List the addresses at which the children have resided, indicating whether they resided with their mother, father, or both.

☞ In paragraph 8, state the full name of the biological mother of the child or children.

☞ In paragraph 9, state the full name of the biological father of the child or children.

☞ In paragraph 13, circle the parent listed that indicates with whom you are requesting the children take residence.

☞ After the section that begins with the word "Wherefore," you will need to circle one of the words in item 2. Circle the word "mother" or "father" (whichever applies to you). If the child has been removed from the Commonwealth of Pennsylvania, also circle the word "Pennsylvania."

☞ Sign your name on the line marked "Name."

☞ Complete the Verification page, which is the last page of the form: Complete the top portion according to the instructions on pages 78–79. Then type in your name on the line in the main paragraph, and date and sign the form on the lines indicated.

If you have a good reason for not notifying your spouse in advance, this form needs to be presented to the judge, along with the ORDER OF COURT. (see form 7, p.213.) To complete the ORDER OF COURT (form 7):

☞ Complete the top portion according to the instructions at the beginning of Chapter 12.

☞ On the second line of the main paragraph, after the word "Plaintiff," type in your name.

☞ On the third line, type in the number of children.

☞ On the fourth line, type in the name or names of the children. The court will fill in the other blank spaces.

Call the secretary for the judge and say that you would like to submit a "Motion for Temporary Custody," and ask how you should do this. The secretary may tell you to come in with your papers at a certain time, to mail them, or to submit them to the prothonotary's office. Simply follow the instructions. If possible, you should notify your spouse of your motion just before you go see the judge, either verbally or by mailing, and file a CERTIFICATE OF SERVICE. (see form 4, p.205.) Otherwise, be prepared to tell the judge why you were unable to notify your spouse. To complete the ORDER OF COURT (form 7), all you need to do is to complete the top portion of the form. The court will either fill in the rest, or tell you how to fill in the rest.

Once you have a signed copy of the ORDER OF COURT (form 7), mail or deliver a copy to your spouse. Then complete a CERTIFICATE OF SERVICE (form 4) to show that you have notified your spouse. If your spouse has not filed any papers with the court yet, you should have the ORDER OF COURT served upon him or her by the sheriff (refer back to Chapter 12 for information on having papers served by the sheriff). It is important to be able to satisfy the court that your spouse knew about the ORDER OF COURT if you need to collect support arrearages, or file contempt proceedings for violation of the custody order.

Modifying Child Custody, Visitation, and Support

14

Child custody, visitation, and child support are issues that may be modified after the divorce is over. The court must apply the relevant legal standard (discussed below) to determine whether modification is in order.

Custody

It is essential that custody be set properly in the initial proceeding. The initial custody determination is made using the thirteen factors discussed on page 19 to determine the "best interests of the child." However, if you later wish to change custody and your spouse does not agree, you must prove that the child is endangered in your ex-spouse's care.

In general, a motion to modify custody may not be brought until a year has passed since the initial custody determination. If there has been a motion to change custody, the parties must wait two years before filing another motion to modify custody, whether or not the change in custody was granted. This is to prevent frequent and harassing filings for custody.

NOTE: *Neither of the above restrictions on filing motions applies if the court finds that there has been interference with visitation, or has reason to believe that the child's present environment may endanger the child.*

If the above qualifications are met, the court may not modify the custody arrangement unless it finds, based on facts that were not known or not available at the time of the previous custody determination, that a change has occurred in the circumstances of the parties or the child. Furthermore, modification must be necessary to serve the best interests of the child. The statute goes on to provide that the court will retain the old custody arrangement unless it finds:

- both parties agree to the modification; .

- the child has been integrated into the family of the petitioner with the consent of the other party; or,

- the child's present environment endangers the child's physical emotional health or impairs the child's emotional development and the harm likely to be caused by a change of environment is outweighed by the advantage of a change to the child.

NOTE: *If you are seeking to change custody, it is essential that you hire an attorney.*

NOTE: *A child at least 16 years of age can seek a change in custody on his/her own. However, it will be the minor's burden to prove that a change of custody would be in his or her best interests at this time.*

COURT'S JURISDICTION

The court that made the original custody or visitation order retains jurisdiction to decide upon modification unless the parties and the child no longer have close ties to the court and the court surrenders its jurisdiction. However, the court with original jurisdiction may refuse to hear the custody case if a child has been wrongfully taken from another state or taken without the consent of the person entitled to custody.

MODIFYING
JOINT CUSTODY

If you are seeking to change a joint custody arrangement the same requirements apply unless the parties agree in writing to applying a different standard or if a party is seeking to move the child out of state.

The Pennsylvania Supreme Court filled the gap and provided that in order to move a child out of state under a joint custody arrangement, the parent seeking to move must prove that it is in the best interests of the child to move out of state. This is a considerably more difficult burden to meet than if the parent seeking to move has sole physical custody.

PARENTING TIME

The court shall modify an order granting or denying parenting time (visitation rights) whenever modification would serve the best interests of the child. The court may not restrict parenting time unless it finds that time is likely to endanger the child's physical or emotional health or impair the child's emotional development or the non-custodial parent has chronically and unreasonably failed to comply with court ordered parenting time. For example, should a one parent consistently withhold custody time from the other parent and attempt to deprive that parent of his or her allotted time with the child(ren), the court may deny or remove rights from the violative or offending parent.

If a party has been denied parenting time, the court may impose a variety of sanctions:

- *compensatory visitation* or *balancing visitation* of the same type and duration as the deprived parenting time (such visitation is used as a form of punishment to the parent who has deprived the other (non-offending) parent of time with the child(ren) by adding extra time with the child(ren) to the deprived parent);

- civil penalty of up to $500; require the depriving party to post a bond;

- award attorney fees and costs;

- require reimbursement of costs incurred due to loss of parenting time; .

- any other remedy the court finds to be in the best interests of the child involved; or,

- in egregious cases, the court may reverse custody.

CHILD SUPPORT

If you believe that circumstances justify a change in child support, there are a number of ways in which you can proceed. Most people enlist the assistance of the child support officer. The child support officer can provide the forms or information necessary to schedule a motion. If you have complex issues or time pressure you may want to hire a private attorney.

If you use a child support officer, the child support officer can compel the parties to disclose information necessary to determine whether a modification of child support is permissible. In addition, parties are required to disclose tax returns every two years, if so requested by the other party. Once the information is obtained the child support officer prepares financial worksheets. Sometimes this is not done until the hearing. Once all the information is provided, it is time to run the child support calculation contained in the form provided in this book. If there is an agreement, the child support officer can prepare an agreement for the parties and the court to sign.

The terms of an order respecting maintenance or support may be modified upon a showing of one or more of the following:

- substantially increased or decreased earnings of a party;

- substantially increased or decreased needs of a party or the child or children that are the subject of these proceedings;

- receipt of assistance under the Pennsylvania Department of Welfare;

- a change in the cost of living for either party as measured by the Federal Bureau of Statistics, any of which makes the terms unreasonable and unfair;

- extraordinary medical expenses of the child not provided for under section the support calculations guidelines; or,

- the addition of work-related or education-related child care expenses of the obligee or a substantial increase or decrease in existing work-related or education-related child care expenses.

In modifying support, the court must consider any needs of the child. It is presumed that there has been a substantial change in circumstances as discussed above and the terms of a current support order shall be presumed to be unreasonable and unfair if:

- the application of the child support guidelines in the statute, to the current circumstances of the parties results in a calculated court order that is at least 20 percent and at least $50 per month higher or lower than the current support order;

- the medical support provisions of the order are not enforceable by the public authority or the custodial parent;

- health coverage ordered is not available to the child for whom the order is established by the parent ordered to provide; or,

- the existing support obligation is in the form of a statement of percentage and not a specific dollar amount.

If the court determines that modification is necessary, the court is to apply the guidelines of Pennsylvania Statutes. The income of a new spouse is not to be considered. In addition, if the paying parent has started to work additional overtime, that is not to be considered in most cases. However, if the paying parent is in *arrears* (monies not paid when due, thus accruing against the party), all of the *net income* (adjusted income that includes all income minus all expenses) from the additional employment must be used to satisfy arrearages until the arrearages are paid in full. Motions for modification of child support are only retroactive to the date a motion is served, except in extraordinary circumstances. For example, retroactivity may not be supported in situations where a parent has voluntarily overpaid support previously without the benefit of a court order. Support retroactivity may be waived or given up by the recipient as a form of good will.

TERMINATING CHILD SUPPORT

A child support order ends automatically upon the *emancipation* (legally becoming an adult) of a child. However, if there are two or more children, the award must be terminated explicitly in the order or by motion. Child Support modification proceedings are generally handled by a magistrate under the Expedited Child Support Process. This process is intended to speed up child support procedures. However, the rules have been modified several times over the past few years. The final rules of the process are not yet available at this writing. The process involving magistrates is more friendly to the unrepresented party, and the traditional rules of evidence do not apply.

CHILDCARE OR DAYCARE COST

Though childcare or daycare is deemed a form of child support, it is not affected by cost-of-living adjustments or included in the guidelines of support calculations. If there has been a substantial change in childcare or daycare costs, either party may seek modification of the support order. If either parent reports that there are no more childcare or daycare costs, the paying parent may petition to reduce the support if that aspect of support had been previously included in your order as of the date of the request. Childcare or daycare costs are generally not factored into the guideline calculations however, they may be negotiated in the support hearing process or used as a potential bargaining tool.

VIOLATION OF THE CUSTODY ORDER AGREEMENT 15

Parents enter Commonwealth courthouses constantly informing the custody officers that the other parent has not returned the child at the scheduled time following a partial custody period and they do not know what to do. When a custody order is violated the law requires the custodial parent/lawful custodian to first demand the return of the child.

If the child is not returned within forty-eight hours, the visitation parent may have committed a crime. If the abducting parent remained within the state it is a *misdemeanor* (minor crime, punishable by a fine or less than one year in prison). If the abducting parent crosses the state line, it is a *felony* (major crime, punishable by more than one year in prison).

If the child has actually been stolen by the other parent you should report this to your local police department immediately. The FBI can be called in to find the fugitive parent and the child as well.

The only exception to this rule is when the child is in clear and present danger (the victim of abuse or abandonment) requiring the non-custodial parent to save them. The non-custodial parent must be ready to prove this clear and present danger and they are required by Pennsylvania law to file a petition within ninety-six hours. In that event, both parents will need a lawyer.

Once an incident like this has happened, you may want to consider modifying the custody order. Modification is discussed in Chapter 14.

FAILURE TO RETURN THE CHILD

If a child is under twelve years of age, it is unlawful to keep that child for more than 48 hours within the Commonwealth of Pennsylvania, or remove the child from the Commonwealth of Pennsylvania for more than 48 hours, after the lawful custodian has demanded the child's return. Pennsylvania has adopted the Uniform Child Custody Jurisdiction Act and the Parental Kidnapping Prevention Act (see Appendix E).

If your child has been removed from the jurisdiction and taken out of state by the non-custodial parent, you have a variety of issues to consider. You can immediately Petition the Court to obtain an Order of Contempt against the non-custodial parent. The Contempt Order should indicate that the child has been removed improperly and illegally from the jurisdiction of the Commonwealth and should instruct enforcement agencies to have the child returned.

JURISDICTION

Jurisdiction is the legal barrier that separates the subjects one court hears from those of another. There are two types of jurisdiction: personal and subject matter. The court must have both types of jurisdiction to hear a case. *Personal jurisdiction*, the power to require a person to appear in court, is discussed in the Service of Process section of this book. To have jurisdiction over your specific custody or visitation case, the court will require one of the following:

- Pennsylvania is the home state of the child (lives in state, goes to school in state) and the parent has sufficient contact with the state (works, votes, lives, pays taxes in Pennsylvania);

- Pennsylvania was the child's home state within the last six months and the parent filing for custody continues to live in Pennsylvania and the child is absent from the state because another person took them out of Pennsylvania claiming custody;

- the child and at least one of the parents have significant connection with Pennsylvania (live, work, go to school here) and in Pennsylvania there are more records and witnesses to give evidence of the child's present or future care, protection, training and personal relationship;

- the child is physically present in Pennsylvania and was abandoned or emergency protection is necessary (the child was threatened or subjected to abuse or neglect);

- no other state would have jurisdiction based on the above mentioned issues;

- another state says Pennsylvania has jurisdiction; or,

- child was removed from Pennsylvania and the Uniform Child Custody Jurisdiction Act does not apply and no other state has jurisdiction, then Pennsylvania will have jurisdiction if:
  - Pennsylvania was where the married couple lived, paid taxes, voted, etc., but the parents are now currently separated or divorced or Pennsylvania was where the marriage contract was last performed;
  - one parent is a resident of Pennsylvania and was a resident when the child was removed; or,
  - court has personal jurisdiction over the parent who has removed the child.

CUSTODY
JURISDICTION

The Uniform Child Custody Jurisdiction Act (UCCJA) has been adopted by Pennsylvania, as well as the other 49 states. This act gives jurisdiction for custody cases to the location that is most closely associated with the child. Within Pennsylvania, the Circuit Court has jurisdiction to hear child custody cases. That court has the power to override any agreement if they believe the agreement is not in the best interest of the child.

In assessing whether you have a case for *contempt* (willful failure to disobey an order of court) and in further assessing whether your child has been improperly removed from the jurisdiction consider the following:

First determine whether any order concerning custody has been entered previously (including paternity, divorce, child protection and/or third-party visitation).

Custody/visitation jurisdiction does not require personal jurisdiction over the parties.

Has the child lived in the same state for the past six months or more (or since birth if the child is younger than six months old)?

- If so, that state is the "home state" under the Uniform Child Custody Jurisdiction Act (UCCJA) and Federal Parental Kidnapping Prevention Act (PKPA), U.S.C.A., Tit. 28, Sec. 1738A, and the action must be filed in that state, or that state must decline to exercise its jurisdiction in favor of another state.

- Should there be a jurisdictional dispute, the judges in both states should confer (UCCJA) and enter a written order on the record. (A reason for declining may be that the other state has more significant connections with the child and his or her family, or that most of the evidence is in the other state.)

Did the child leave his or her "home state" within the past six months?

- If so, the "recent home state" (UCCJA) has jurisdiction until the child has been away in excess of six months.

- File your Contempt Petition in the "recent home state" immediately, before it loses jurisdictional priority.

- File an affidavit regarding the child's residence for the past five years, including where the child has lived and with whom, whether any other custody or visitation actions are pending, and whether anyone else has or claims to have custody or visitation rights (UCCJA).

Have the court recite the basis for its jurisdiction in every custody or visitation order.

- Unless the home state declined its jurisdiction, an order entered in any other state enforceable elsewhere (PKPA) and may be subject to reversal on appeal. Generally, the PKPA supercedes and takes preference over the UCCJA (the PKPA has a stronger preference for "home state").

- The parties may not agree to custody jurisdiction. (Custody jurisdiction is considered "subject matter jurisdiction" and is therefore a jurisdictional requirement which cannot be waived by the parties.).

The matter is fairly simple if the child has always lived in the same state—that state has jurisdiction. If another state has entered an order, the PKPA is of jurisdiction.

MODIFICATION OF JURISDICTION

The Federal PKPA preempts the state UCCJA and applies to all custody and visitation cases, even those that do not involve kidnapping. For jurisdictional purposes, it doesn't matter whether the new action is seeking a direct modification; if it has the effect of modifying a previous order, even indirectly, PKPA jurisdiction attaches.

The state that entered the most recent order in accordance with the PKPA has exclusive continuing modification jurisdiction as long as the child or one party continues to reside in that state and that state has jurisdiction under its own law—some states, such as Texas, statutorily give up jurisdiction when the child has resided elsewhere for six months.

Obtain copies of all custody and visitation orders from all states. Trace jurisdiction for each state to make certain the order was entered by the home state or a state to which the home state had declined jurisdiction, and that the order otherwise complied with the PKPA.

If you wish to have a state modify the order of another state, you first must ask the court that issued the earlier decree (the state that has continuing jurisdiction) to decline to exercise jurisdiction.

The UCCJA recognizes emergency jurisdiction, but it is temporary jurisdiction only; permanent orders must be entered in the proper state. Consider filing in the proper state initially if you can obtain relief quickly enough

EMERGENCY REQUEST FOR JURISDICTION

If you file based solely on emergency jurisdiction, state in your pleading (legal document filed in a court proceeding) that you are seeking temporary relief only until application can be made to the state with superior jurisdiction. Request that the judges in the two states communicate (UCCJA) and send a copy of the pleading to the court with superior jurisdiction (so that the judge will be less likely to be offended by the filing and less likely to hold it against your client).

ENFORCEMENT OF JURISDICTION

Enforcement requires personal jurisdiction; an order entered in conformity with the PKPA is entitled to enforcement nationwide without modification. Although the UCCJA does not require registration or filing of a foreign order as a prerequisite to enforcement, some law enforcement officers refuse to enforce foreign court orders in the Commonwealth.

Should you require aid in locating a child who has been improperly removed from the jurisdiction in which you reside, you may find aid through the following agency:

National Center for Missing and Exploited Children
2101 Wilson Boulevard, Suite 550
Arlington, VA 22201
703-235-3900
Hotline: 1-800-843-5678

SECTION 6:
THE LEGAL SYSTEM AND LAWYERS

COMMONWEALTH LEGAL SYSTEM 16

This chapter will present to you a broad-spectrum introduction to the legal system. There is information that you must comprehend and fully understand in order to move though the custody or support process (or to assist your lawyer in the effective handling of your case), and to proceed through any encounter with the legal system with a minimum of tension. The following are a few of the truths, realities, and certainties we observe within our system. If you fail to learn or to accept these truths and certainties, you will undergo a great deal of unnecessary anxiety and frustration.

RULES AND PROCEDURE, GENERALLY

Our legal system is a system of rules. There are three basic categories of rules:

1. *Rules of law.* These are the basic substance of the law, such as a law telling a judge how to go about dividing your property.

2. *Rules of procedure.* These outline how matters are to be handled in the courts, such as requiring court papers to be in a certain form, or filed within a certain time.

3. *Rules of evidence.* These set forth the manner in which facts are to be proven.

The fiction is that these rules allow each side to present evidence most favorable to that side, and an independent person or persons (such as the judge or jury) will figure out the truth. Then, certain legal principles will be applied to that "truth" which will give a fair resolution of the dispute. These legal principles are supposed to be relatively unchanging so that we can all know what will happen in any given situation and can plan our lives accordingly. This will provide order and predictability to our society. Any change in the legal principles is supposed to occur slowly, so that the expected behavior in our society is not confused from day-to-day. Unfortunately, the system does not really work this way. What follows are only some of the problems in the real legal system.

The fact is that contrary to the way in which it may appear, legal rules are not made just to complicate matters and confuse everyone. They are attempts to make the system fair and just. They have been developed over hundreds of years, and in most cases, they do make sense. Unfortunately, our efforts to find fairness and justice have resulted in a complex set of rules. The legal system affects our lives in important ways, and it is not a game. However, it can be compared to a game in some ways. The rules are designed to apply to all people and in all cases. Sometimes, the rules do not seem to provide a fair result in a certain situation, but the rules are still followed. Just as a referee can make a bad call, so can a judge. There are also cases where one side wins by deceitful means.

Many young lawyers are shocked to discover that judges do not always follow the rules. After spending three years in law school learning legal theory, and after spending countless hours preparing for a hearing and having all of the law on your side, you find that the judge simply is not going to attribute any attention to legal theories or to the law. Many judges are going to make a decision on what they think *seems* fair under the circumstances. This somewhat morality based judging is actually being taught in some law schools at present. Unfortunately, that which seems fair to a particular judge may depend upon his or her personal ideas and philosophy.

Example: There is no provision in the divorce code that gives one parent priority in child custody. However, many judges believe that a child is usually better off with his or her mother. All other aspects of the case being equal, such judges will still find an avenue by which to justify awarding custody to the mother.

Even lawyers become annoyed and discouraged at the length of time it can take to get a case completed. Whatever your situation, things will take longer than you expect. Patience is required to get through the system with a minimum of stress. Do not let your frustration show. No matter what happens in your case, remain calm, be ever courteous, and be patient.

Simply because your friend's case proceeded in a certain way does not mean that your case will garner the same result. The judge assigned to your case can make a significant difference, and more often, the circumstances particular to each individual will make a difference. Just as no two fingerprints are alike, it can be said that no two family law matters are alike. Simply because your co-worker makes the same income as you make and he or she has the same number of children, you can not assume that you will be ordered to pay the same amount of child support. There are typically other circumstances about which your co-worker does not tell you, and possibly other aspects of the case that your co-worker does not fully understand.

THE PLAYERS

The law and the legal system are often compared to games, and just like games, it is important to know the players.

THE JUDGE

The judge has the power to decide how your custody matter will proceed, how custody of the children will be arranged, and how much the other will pay for child support. The judge is the last person you want to make angry. In general, judges have large caseloads and like it best when your case can be concluded quickly and without hassle. This means that the more you and your spouse agree upon, and the more complete your paperwork, the more you will please the judge. Most likely, your only direct contact with the judge will be at certain hearings, which may last as little as five minutes. (See Chapter 7 for more about how to deal with the judge.)

JUDGE'S SECRETARY

The judge's secretary may set certain hearing dates for the judge and can frequently answer many of your questions about the procedure and what the judge would like or require in your case. Clearly, you do not wish to make an enemy of the secretary. This means that you do not call the judge's secretary repeatedly, and you do not ask too many questions. A few questions are considered acceptable, and you may want to start off saying that you just want to make sure you have everything in order for the judge. You will get much farther by being polite than by arguing or being demanding.

PROTHONOTARY

In most counties in the Commonwealth of Pennsylvania, custody cases are filed with the office of the prothonotary (in most states, the prothonotary is called the court clerk). In a few places, such as Philadelphia, cases are filed with the office of the Family Court Clerk.

NOTE: *Unless a significant distinction between the prothonotary and clerk is noted, any reference to the prothonotary should also be considered as a reference to the clerk in those counties.*

Where the secretary usually works for only one judge, the prothonotary handles the files for all of the judges. The prothonotary's office is the central place where all of the court files are kept. The prothonotary files your court papers and keeps the official records of your divorce. Most people who work in the prothonotary's office are friendly and helpful. While they cannot give you legal advice (such as advising you what to say in your court papers), they can help explain the system and the procedures (such as telling you what type of papers must be filed). The prothonotary has the power to accept or reject your papers, so you do not want to anger the prothonotary. If the prothonotary tells you to change something in your papers, just change it. Do not argue or complain.

LAWYERS
Lawyers serve as guides through the legal system. They try to guide their own client, while trying to confuse, manipulate, or out-maneuver their opponent. In dealing with your spouse's lawyer (if he or she has one), try to be polite. You will not get anywhere by being antagonistic. Generally, the lawyer is just doing his or her job to get the best situation for his or her client. Some lawyers cannot be reasoned with, and you should not try. If your spouse gets one of these lawyers, it is a good idea for you to get a lawyer also. Chapter 3 will provide more information to help you decide if you need a lawyer.

This book will serve as your map of the trail through the legal system. In most cases, the dangers along the way are relatively small. If you start getting lost, or the dangers seem to be getting worse, you can always hire a lawyer to jump to your aid. You may wish to contact the Lawyer's Referral Service in your area. Your county bar association can guide you in this regard. The following sections give you a general overview of the law and procedures involved in moving through the custody, visitation, and support systems. To most people, the law appears very complicated and confusing. Fortunately, many areas of the law can be broken down into simple and logical steps. Custody is one of those areas.

RESEARCHING THE LAW

This book has been designed so that you do not need to do research. However, if you need, or want, to find out more about the custody and support law in Pennsylvania, this section will give you some guidance.

STATUTES   The main source of information on Pennsylvania divorce, custody, and support law is the Pennsylvania Divorce Code. This is the portion of the laws passed by the Pennsylvania Legislature (the Pennsylvania Statutes) that specifically relates to custody and support cases. Selected portions of the Code are found in Appendix A of this book. The complete code may be found as an individual book that only contains the Pennsylvania Divorce Code, or in Title 23 of Purdon's Pennsylvania Consolidated Statutes Annotated (which is discussed further below). You can usually find it at the public library, although check to be sure they have the most recent edition. You may also find it at your nearest law library, which is often located in your county courthouse or at a university campus where a law school is located.

All of the laws passed by the Pennsylvania Legislature may be found in a set of books titled Purdon's Pennsylvania Consolidated Statutes Annotated. These books contain all of the statutes (not just those relating to "divorce, custody and support" cases). Each statute is followed by summaries (called annotations) of court cases, which discuss and interpret that section of the statutes.

CASES   In addition to the laws passed by the legislature, law is also made by the decisions of the judges in various cases each year. To find this case law you will need to go to a law library. Each county has a law library connected with the court, so you can ask the prothonotary where the law library is located. Also, law schools have libraries, which may be open to the public. Do not be afraid to ask the librarians for assistance. They cannot give you legal advice, but they can tell you where the books are located. Case law may be found in Purdon's Pennsylvania Consolidated Statutes Annotated, as well as in the source listed below:

The Law—Purdon's Pennsylvania Consolidated Statutes Annotated (PA Cons. Stat. Ann.), Title 23 (Tit.), Section (Sec) 5303.

DIGESTS   The Pennsylvania Digest is a set of books that give short summaries of cases, and the place where you can find the court 's full written opinion. The digest is arranged alphabetically by subject. Find the chapter on custody then look for the headings of the subject you want.

REPORTERS   The Atlantic Reporter is where the appeals courts publish their written opinions on the cases they hear. There are two series of the Atlantic Reporter. The older cases are found in the Atlantic Reporter (abbreviated "A."), and newer cases are found in the Atlantic Reporter 2d Series ("A.2d").

Example: If the digest gives you a reference to "McMillen v. Mcmillen, 602 A.2d845," this tells you that the case titled "McMillen v. McMillen" can be found by going to Volume 602 (the first number) of the Atlantic Reporter 2d Series (A.2d), and turning to page 845 (the second number).

RULES OF COURT   The Pennsylvania Rules of Court are the rules that are applied in the various courts in Pennsylvania, and they also contain some approved forms. These rules mainly deal with forms and procedures. You would be primarily concerned with the Rules of Civil Procedure.

UCCJA   The Uniform Child Custody Jurisdiction Act, known as the UCCJA, is the guide for all custody matters. It makes uniform and standardized the application of custody rules and enforcement of custody orders across the United States.

Child Custody—(Pa. Cons. Stat. Ann, Title 23 Sec. 5303 and 5304). The court must consider the preference of the child as well as any other factors that legitimately impact the child's physical, intellectual, and emotional well-being. A best interests of the child standard is applied. An Order for Shared Custody may be awarded by the court when it is in the best interests of the child; upon application of one or both parents; when the parties have agreed to an award of shared custody; or in the discretion of the court. In a Sole Custody or Visitation Order, the court must consider which parent is more likely to encourage, permit, and allow frequent and continuing contact and physical access between the non-custodial parent and the child. However, a court will consider each parent and adult household member's present or past violent or abusive behavior in making an award of custody.

Child Support—(Pennsylvania Rules of Civil Procedure 1910.16-1 to 1910.16-5.) The guidelines are based upon a percentage of adjusted net income of the parents. Certain proportional adjustments are made based upon permitted additional expenses, such as healthcare. There are currently five (5) percentages applicable in the guidelines based upon the number of children and income levels. The proportionate percentage of each parents' obligation is then determined, and the non-custodial parent pays his or her share to the custodial parent. There are special guideline calculations for divided or split custody arrangements. Deviations are permitted under specific situations (e.g.: for unusual needs, extraordinary medical expenses). Modifications are permitted upon a material and substantial change in the support amount.

PRACTICE
MANUALS

In addition to the sources mentioned on the previous pages, you may also find practice manuals which are books, or sets of books, covering specific areas of the law. For example, there are practice manuals for drunk driving cases, probate, bankruptcy, and custody. A Custody of Family Practice manual will explain the law, and usually provide sample forms. The law librarians can help you locate such books.

LAWYERS 17

Whether you need an attorney will depend upon many factors, such as how comfortable you feel handling the matter yourself, whether your situation is more complicated than usual, and how much opposition you get from your spouse as to the custody arrangements or support payments. It may be advisable to hire an attorney if you encounter a judge with a hostile attitude, or if your spouse gets a lawyer who wants to fight. There are no court-appointed lawyers in custody cases, so if you want an attorney, you will have to hire one or seek aid from the local volunteer legal aid agency. This may be available to you only if you meet certain reduced means criteria in income.

A very general rule is that you should consider hiring an attorney whenever you reach a point where you no longer feel comfortable representing yourself. This point will vary greatly with each person, so there is no easy way to be more definite.

A more appropriate question is: "Do you want a lawyer?" The next section will discuss some of the "pros" and "cons" of hiring a lawyer, and some of the elements you may wish to consider in making this decision.

Determining if You want a Lawyer

One of the first questions you will want to consider, and most likely the reason you are reading this book, is: How much will an attorney cost? Attorneys come in all ages, shapes, sizes, sexes, racial, and ethnic groups and also price ranges. For a very rough estimate, you can expect an attorney to charge anywhere from $500 to $2,000 for a custody matter. Lawyers usually charge an hourly rate for representation ranging from about $95 to $300 per hour. Most new (and therefore less expensive) attorneys would be quite capable of handling a simple custody matter or support case, but, if your situation became more complicated, you would probably prefer a more experienced lawyer. As a general rule, you can expect the cost to be more than what you think it will cost at the beginning.

ADVANTAGES OF HAVING A LAWYER

There are some advantages to hiring a lawyer. Judges and other attorneys may take you more seriously. Most judges prefer both parties to have attorneys. They feel this helps the case move in a more orderly fashion because both sides will know the procedures and relevant issues. Persons representing themselves very often waste a lot of time on matters that have absolutely no bearing on the outcome of the case. A lawyer will serve as a "buffer" between you and your spouse. This can lead to a quicker passage through the system by reducing the chance for emotions to take control and confuse the issues.

For the same reasons that are listed above, attorneys prefer to deal with other attorneys. However, if you become familiar with this book, and conduct yourself in a calm and proper manner, you should have no trouble. (Proper courtroom manners are discussed in Chapter 7.)

You can let your lawyer worry about all of the details. By having an attorney, you need only become generally familiar with the contents of this book, as it will be your attorney's job to file the proper papers in the correct form, and to deal with the prothonotary, the judge, the *process server* (person who hand delivers filed court documents to a party involved in a legal matter), your spouse, and your spouse's attorney.

Lawyers provide professional assistance with problems. In the event your case is complicated, or suddenly becomes complicated, it is an advantage to have an attorney who is familiar with your case. It can also be comforting to have a lawyer to turn to for advice and answers to your questions.

ADVANTAGES OF
REPRESENTING
YOURSELF

On the other hand, there are also advantages to representing yourself. Not only do you save the cost of a lawyer, but sometimes judges feel more sympathetic toward a person not represented by an attorney. This sometimes results in the unrepresented person being allowed a certain amount of leeway with the procedure rules.

The procedure may be faster. Two of the most frequent complaints about lawyers received by the bar association involve delay in completing the case and failure to return phone calls. Most lawyers have a heavy caseload, which sometimes results in lapses of time in addressing cases. If you are following the progress of your own case you will be able to push it along the system diligently.

CHOOSING A LAWYER

Selecting a lawyer is a two-step process. First, you need to decide with which attorney you will make an appointment. Then you need to decide if you wish to hire (retain) that attorney.

ASKING A
FRIEND

A common, and frequently the best, way to find a lawyer is to ask someone you know to recommend one to you. This is especially helpful if the lawyer represented your friend in a custody, support or other family law matter.

LAWYER
REFERRAL
SERVICE

You can find a referral service by looking in the Yellow Pages phone directory under "Attorney Referral Services" or "attorneys." This is a service, usually operated by a bar association, that is designed to match a client with an attorney handling cases in the area of law the client needs. The referral service does not guarantee the quality of work, nor the level of experience or ability of the attorney. Finding a lawyer in this manner will at least connect you with one who is practicing in the area of family law and probably has some experience in this area.

YELLOW PAGES

Check under the heading for "Attorneys" in the yellow pages phone directory. Many of the lawyers and law firms will place display ads indicating their areas of practice, and educational backgrounds. Look for firms or lawyers that indicate they practice in areas such as "divorce", "family law", or "domestic relations". Big ads are not necessarily indicative of expertise. Keep in mind that some lawyers, and often the best lawyers, do not need to advertise.

ASKING
ANOTHER
LAWYER

If you have used the services of an attorney in the past for some other matter (for example, a real estate closing, traffic ticket, or a will) you may want to call and ask if he or she could refer you to an attorney whose ability in the area of family law is respected.

From your search, you should select three to five lawyers worthy of further consideration. Your first step will be to call each attorney's office, explain that you are interested in seeking a divorce, and ask the following questions:

- Does the attorney (or law firm) handle this type of matter?

- What is the fee range and what is the cost of an initial consultation? (Do not expect to get a definite answer on a fee, but the attorney may be able to give you a range or an hourly rate. You will probably need to meet with the lawyer for anything more detailed.)

- How soon can you get an appointment?

Most offices require you to make an appointment. Once you get in contact with the attorney at the appointment, ask the following questions:

- How much will it cost?

- How will the fee be paid?

- How long has the attorney been in practice?

- How long has the attorney been in practice in Pennsylvania?

- What percentage of the attorney's cases involve divorce cases or other family law matters? (Do not expect an exact answer, but you should get a rough estimate that is at least twenty percent.)

- How long will it take? (Do not expect an exact answer, but the attorney should be able to give you an average range and discuss things that may make a difference.)

If you get acceptable answers to these questions, it is time to ask yourself the following questions about the lawyer:

- Do you feel comfortable talking to the lawyer?

- Is the lawyer friendly toward you?

- Does the lawyer seem confident in himself or herself?

- Does the lawyer seem to be straight-forward with you, and able to explain issues so you understand?

If you get satisfactory answers to all of these questions, you probably have a lawyer with whom you will be happy to work. Most clients are happiest with an attorney with whom they feel comfortable.

Selecting any attorney is not easy. As this section shows, it is hard to know whether you are selecting an attorney with whom you will be happy.

You may want to look for an attorney who will be willing to accept an hourly fee to answer your questions and give you help as you need it. This way you will save some legal costs, but still receive some professional assistance. You will also establish a relationship with an attorney who will be somewhat familiar with your case in the event things become complicated and you need a full-time lawyer.

WORKING WITH A LAWYER

In general, you will work best with your attorney if you keep an open, honest, and friendly attitude. Also, consider the following suggestions.

ASKING THE LAWYER QUESTIONS

If you want to know something or if you do not understand something, ask your attorney. If you do not understand the answer, tell your attorney and ask him or her to explain it again. You should not be embarrassed to ask questions. Many people who say they had a bad experience with a lawyer either did not ask enough questions or had a lawyer who would not take the time to explain things to them. If your lawyer is not taking the time to explain what he or she is doing, it may be time to look for a new lawyer.

Many lawyers operate on the old principle of the squeaking wheel gets the oil. Work on a case tends to be put off until a deadline is near, an emergency develops, or the client calls. There is a reason for this. Many lawyers take more cases than can be effectively handled in order to earn the income they desire. Your task is to become a squeaking wheel that does not squeak too much. Whenever you talk to your lawyer ask the following questions:

- What is the next step?

- When do you expect it to be done?

- When should I talk to you next?

Call your lawyer if you do not hear anything when you expect. Do not remind your lawyer of the missed call; just ask how things are going.

TELLING THE LAWYER EVERYTHING

Anything you tell your attorney is confidential. An attorney can lose his or her license to practice if he or she reveals information without your permission. So do not hold back. Tell your lawyer everything, even if it does not seem important to you. There are many things that seem unimportant to a non-attorney, but can change the outcome of a case. Also, do not hold something back because you are afraid it will hurt your case. It will definitely hurt your case if your lawyer does not find out about it until he or she hears it in court from your spouse's attorney. But if your lawyer knows in advance, he or she can plan to eliminate or reduce damage to your case.

LISTENING TO THE LAWYER'S ANSWERS

Listen to what your lawyer tells you about the law and the system. It will do you no good to argue because the law or the system does not work the way you think it should. For example, if your lawyer tells you that the judge can not hear your case for two weeks, do not try demanding that he or she set a hearing tomorrow. By refusing to accept reality, you are only setting yourself up for disappointment. Remember, it is not your attorney's fault that the system is not perfect, or that the law does not say what you would like it to say.

BEING PATIENT

The advice to be patient applies both to being patient with the system (which is often slow as we discussed earlier), as well as being patient with your attorney. Do not expect your lawyer to return your phone call within an hour. Your lawyer may not be able to return it the same day. Most lawyers are very busy. It is rare that an attorney can maintain a full caseload and still make each client feel as if he or she is the only client. Despite the popular trend toward "lawyer-bashing," you should remember that many lawyers are good people who wish to aid and assist the public.

SPEAKING WITH THE SECRETARY	Your lawyer's secretary can be a valuable source of information. Be friendly and get to know the secretary. Often he or she will be able to answer your questions, and you will not get a bill for the time you talk to the secretary.
COMMUNICATING WITH YOUR SPOUSE	It is your lawyer's job to communicate with your spouse, or with your spouse's lawyer. Let your lawyer do his or her job. Many lawyers have had clients lose or damage their cases when the client decides to say or do something on their own.
BEING ON TIME	The advice to be on time applies to both appointments with your lawyer, and to court hearings, scheduling is very important.

FIRING A LAWYER

If you can no longer work with your lawyer, it is time to either go it alone or get a new attorney. You will need to send your lawyer a letter stating that you no longer desire his or her services and are discharging him or her from your case. Also state that you will be coming by his or her office the following day to pick up your file. The attorney does not have to give you his or her own notes or other work he or she has in progress, but he or she must give you the essential contents of your file (such as copies of papers already filed or prepared and billed for, and any documents that you provided). If the lawyer refuses to give you your file, for any reason, contact the Pennsylvania Bar about filing a complaint, or grievance, against the lawyer. You will, however, need to settle any remaining fees charged for work that has already been done by the lawyer.

Glossary

A

abandon. To intentionally and permanently give up, surrender, leave, desert, or relinquish all interest and ownership in property, a home or other premises, a right of way, or even a spouse, family, or children. To abandon children can mean to have no contact and give no support for a year or more.

accept. To approve of and intend to keep. Accept is often used in reference to a payment that is late or not complete, or accepting the "service" (delivery) of legal papers.

acceptance. Receiving something from another with the intent to keep it, and/or showing that this was based on a previous agreement.

acceptance of service. Agreement by a defendant (or his/her attorney) in a legal action to accept a complaint or other petition (like divorce papers) without having the sheriff or process server show up at the door.

accrue. Growing or adding to, such as interest on a debt or investment which continues to accumulate.

acknowledgment. The section at the end of a document where a notary public verifies that the signer of the document states he/she actually signed it.

action. A lawsuit in which one party (or parties) sues another.

admit. To state something is true when answering a complaint filed in a lawsuit. The defendant will admit or deny each allegation in his or her answer filed with the court.

adopt. To take on the relationship of parent of another person, particularly (but not necessarily) a minor, by official legal action.

adoption. The taking of a child into one's family, creating a parent to child relationship, and giving him or her all the rights and privileges of one's own child, including the right to inherit as if the child were the adopter's natural child.

adultery. Consensual sexual relations when one of the participants is legally married to someone else. In some states it is still a crime and in many states it is grounds for divorce for the spouse of the married adulterer. The criminal charges are almost never brought, and in those states in which there is no-fault divorce (or dissolution), adultery is legally not relevant.

affidavit. Any written document in which the signer swears under oath before a notary public or someone authorized to take oaths (like a County Clerk), that the statements in the document are true.

agreement. Any meeting of the minds, even without legal obligation and/or in law, another name for a contract including all the elements of a legal contract: offer, acceptance, and consideration (payment or performance), based on specific terms.

alimony. Support paid by one ex-spouse to the other as ordered by a court in a divorce (dissolution) case. Alimony is also called "spousal support" in California and some other states.

allegation. Statement of claimed fact contained in a complaint (a written pleading filed to begin a lawsuit), a criminal charge, or an affirmative defense (part of the written answer to a complaint).

allege. To claim a fact is true, commonly in a complaint which is filed to commence a lawsuit, in an "affirmative defense" to a complaint, in a criminal charge of the commission of a crime or any claim.

amend. To alter or change by adding, subtracting, or substituting.

antenuptial (prenuptial) agreement. A written contract between two people who are about to marry, setting out the terms of possession of assets, treatment of future earnings, control of the property of each, and potential division if the marriage is later dissolved.

appeal. To ask a higher court to reverse the decision of a trial court after final judgment ,or other legal ruling.

appraiser. A professional who appraises the value of property. Some specialize in real property, and others in other types of assets from rugs to rings.

appreciation. The increase in value through the natural course of events as distinguished from improvements or additions.

arrears. Money not paid when due, usually the sum of a series of unpaid amounts, such as rent, installments on an account or promissory note, or monthly child support. Sometimes these are called "arrearages."

asset. Any item or property with monetary value, including those with only sentimental value (particularly in the estates of the dead). Assets are shown in balance sheets of businesses and inventories of probate estates.

B

bifurcate. The order or ruling of a judge that one issue in a case can be tried to a conclusion or a judgment given on one phase of the case without trying all aspects of the matter. A typical example is when the judge will grant a divorce judgment without hearing evidence or making a ruling on such issues as division of marital property, child custody or spousal support (alimony).

breach of contract. Failing to perform any term of a contract, written or oral, without a legitimate legal excuse. This may include not completing a job, not paying in full or on time, failure to deliver all the goods, substituting inferior or significantly different goods, not providing a bond when required, being late without excuse, or any act which shows the party will not complete the work.

C

capital gains. The difference between the sale price and the original cost (plus improvements) of property.

case law. Reported decisions of appeals courts and other courts that make new interpretations of the law and, therefore, can be cited as precedents.

child. A person's natural offspring, or, generally a person 14 years and under.

child custody. Physical and/or legal control and responsibility of a minor (child) under 18 determined by the court. Child custody can be decided by a local court in a divorce or if a child, relative, close friend or state agency questions whether one or both parents is unfit, absent, dead, in prison or dangerous to the child's well-being.

child support. Funds ordered by the court to be paid by one parent to the custodial parent of a minor child after divorce (dissolution) or separation.

civil procedure. The complex and often confusing body of rules and regulations set out in both state (usually Code of Civil Procedure) and federal (Federal Code of Procedure) laws which establish the format under which civil lawsuits are filed, pursued and tried.

claim. To make a demand for money, property, or enforcement of a right provided by law.

common-law marriage. An agreement between a man and woman to live together as husband and wife without any legal formalities, followed and/or preceded by cohabitation on a regular basis (usually for seven years). Common-law marriage is legal in thereby recognizing a marriage for purposes of giving the other party the rights of a spouse, including inheritance or employee benefits.

complaint. The first document filed with the court (actually with the county clerk or clerk of the court) by a person or entity claiming legal rights against another. Complaints are pleadings and must be drafted carefully (usually by an attorney) to properly state the factual as well as legal basis for the claim.

compromise. An agreement between opposing parties to settle a dispute or reach a settlement in which each gives some ground, rather than continue the dispute or go to trial.

conjugal rights. A spouse's so-called "rights" to the comforts and companionship from his/her mate, meaning sexual relations.

consent. To agree with another's proposition, or to voluntarily agree to an act or proposal of another.

consent decree. An order of a judge based upon an agreement, almost always put in writing, between the parties to a lawsuit instead of continuing the case through trial or hearing.

contempt of court. There are essentially two types of contempt: a) being rude, disrespectful to the judge or other attorneys or causing a disturbance in the courtroom, particularly after being warned by the judge; or, b) willful failure to obey an order of the court. (This latter can include failure to pay child support or alimony.)

contingent fee. Fee to a lawyer which will be due and payable only if there is a successful conclusion of the legal work, usually winning or settling a lawsuit in favor of the client (particularly in negligence cases), or collecting funds due with or without filing a lawsuit.

continuance. Postponement of a date of a trial, hearing or other court appearance to a later fixed date by order of the court, or upon a stipulation (legal agreement) by the attorneys and approved by the court or (where local rules permit) by the clerk of the court.

counselor. A licensed attorney or lawyer.

court. The judge, as in "The court rules in favor of the plaintiff", or any official tribunal (court) presided over by a judge or judges in which legal issues and claims are heard and determined. In the United States there are essentially two systems: *federal courts* and *state courts*. Common Pleas Courts are the first level of court in the Commonwealth of Pennsylvania. They are the county court from which all cases may be able to be appealed to a higher level court.

court calendar. List of matters to be heard or set for trial or hearing by a court.

court costs. Fees for expenses that the courts pass on to attorneys, who then pass them on to their clients or to the losing party. (Court costs usually include: filing fees, charges for serving summons and subpoenas, court reporter charges for depositions, court transcripts, and copying papers and exhibits.)

court docket. *(See docket.)*

credibility. Whether testimony is worthy of belief, based on competence of the witness and likelihood that it is true. Unless the testimony is contrary to other known facts or is extremely unlikely based on human experience, the test of credibility is purely subjective.

cross-examination. Opportunity for the attorney (or an unrepresented party) to ask questions in court of a witness who has testified in a trial on behalf of the opposing party.

custody. In domestic relations (divorce, dissolution), a court's determination of which parent (or other appropriate party) should have physical and/or legal control and responsibility for a minor child.

D

decree. Synonymous with judgment except in some specific areas of the law.

default judgment. If a defendant in a lawsuit fails to respond to a complaint in the time set by law (commonly 20 or 30 days), then the plaintiff (who is suing) can request that the default (failure) be entered into the court record by the clerk.

defendant. Party sued in a civil lawsuit or the party charged with a crime in a criminal prosecution. In some types of cases (such as divorce) a defendant may be called a respondent.

direct examination. First questioning of a witness during a trial or deposition (testimony out of court), as distinguished from cross-examination by opposing attorneys and redirect examination when the witness is again questioned by the original attorney.

dissolution. A modern term for divorce, officially used in California since 1970 and symbolic of the no-fault, non-confrontational approach to dissolving a marriage.

distribution. Act of dividing up the assets of an estate or trust, or paying out profits or assets of a corporation or business according to the ownership percentages.

District Courts. Federal trial courts are District Courts in one or more districts per state, over which there are District Courts of Appeal (usually three-judge panels) to hear appeals from judgments of the District Courts within the "circuit."

docket. Cases on a court calendar.

domestic relations. Polite term for the legal field of divorce, dissolution, annulment, child custody, child support and alimony.

domestic violence. Continuing crime and problem of the physical beating of a wife, girlfriend, and/or children, usually by the woman's male partner (although it can also be female violence against a male.)

domicile. Place where a person has his/her permanent principal home to which he/she returns or intends to return.

divorce. Termination of a marriage by legal action, requiring a petition or complaint for divorce.

E

equitable. Just, based on fairness, and not upon legal technicalities.

exhibit. Document or object (including a photograph) introduced as evidence during a trial.

expert testimony. Opinions stated during trial or deposition (testimony under oath before trial) by a specialist qualified as an expert on a subject relevant to a lawsuit or a criminal case.

expert witness. Person who is a specialist in a subject, often technical, who may present his/her expert opinion without having been a witness to any occurrence relating to the lawsuit or criminal case.

F

fact. Actual thing or happening, which must be proved at trial by presentation of evidence and which is evaluated by the finder of fact (a jury in a jury trial, or by the judge if he/she sits without a jury).

federal court. The basic federal court system has jurisdiction over cases involving federal statutes, constitutional questions, actions between citizens of different states, and certain other types of cases. There are also special federal courts such as bankruptcy and tax courts with appeals directed to the District Courts.

H

hearing. Any proceeding before a judge or other magistrate without a jury in which evidence and/or argument is presented to determine some issue of fact or both issues of fact and law.

hearsay. Second-hand evidence in which the witness is not telling what he or she knows personally, but what others have said to him or her.

hearsay rule. Testimony or documents that quote persons not in court are not admissible as evidence.

I

income. Money, goods or other economic benefit received.

J

joint custody. In divorce actions, a decision by the court (often upon agreement of the parents) that the parents will share custody of a child.

joint. Referring to property, rights or obligations that are united, undivided and shared by two or more persons or entities.

jurisdiction. Authority given by law to a court to try cases and rule on legal matters within a particular geographic area and/or over certain types of legal cases.

L

legal separation. Court-decreed right to live apart, with the rights and obligations of divorced persons, but without divorce. The parties are still married and cannot remarry.

legal services. Work performed by a lawyer for a client.

M

marriage. Joining of a male and female in matrimony by a person qualified by law to perform the ceremony (a minister, priest, judge, justice of the peace or some similar official), after having obtained a valid marriage license (which requires a blood test for venereal disease in about a third of the states and a waiting period from one to five days in several).

matter of record. Anything, including testimony, evidence, rulings and sometimes arguments, which has been recorded by the court reporter or court clerk.

minor. Anyone under 18 in almost all states.

N

negotiation. 1) Transfer of a check, promissory note, bill of exchange or other negotiable instrument to another for money, goods, services or other benefit; or, 2) the give-and-take discussion or conference in an attempt to reach an agreement or settle a dispute.

no fault divorce. Divorces (dissolutions) in which neither spouse is required to prove "fault" or marital misconduct on the part of the other.

notary public. Person authorized by the state in which the person resides to administer oaths (swearings to truth of a statement), take acknowledgments, certify documents and to take depositions if the notary is also a court reporter.

O

objection. Lawyer's protest to the legal propriety of a question that has been asked of a witness by the opposing attorney, with the purpose of making the trial judge decide if the question can be asked.

offer. Specific proposal to enter into an agreement with another.

order to show cause. Judge's written mandate that a party appear in court on a certain date and give reasons, legal and/or factual, (show cause) why a particular order should not be made.

P

parent. Lawful or natural father or mother of a person. The word does not mean grandparent or ancestor, but can include an adoptive parent as a replacement for a natural parent.

parental neglect. Crime consisting of acts or omissions of a parent (including a stepparent, adoptive parent or someone who, in practical terms, serves in a parent's role) which endangers the health and life of a child or fails to take steps necessary to the proper raising of a child.

pendente lite. Latin term for "awaiting the litigation (lawsuit)."

personal property. *(See personalty.)*

personalty. Movable assets (things, including animals) which are not real property, money or investments.

plaintiff. Party who initiates a lawsuit by filing a complaint with the clerk of the court against the defendant(s) demanding damages, performance and/or court determination of rights.

pleading. 1) Every legal document filed in a lawsuit, petition, motion and/or hearing, including complaint, petition, answer, demurrer, motion, declaration and memorandum of points and authorities (written argument citing precedents and statutes; 2).the act of preparing and presenting legal documents and arguments.

process server. Person who hand delivers filed court documentation to a party involvd in a legal matter or law suit.

R

real property. Land, structures, firmly attached and integrated equipment (such as light fixtures or a well pump), anything growing on the land. "Interests" in real property may include the right to future ownership (remainder), right to occupy for a period of time (tenancy or life estate), the right to drill for oil, the right to get the property back (a reversion) if it is no longer used for its current purpose (such as use for a hospital, school or city hall), use of airspace (condominium) or an easement across another's property.

relevant. Having some reasonable connection with, and in regard to evidence in trial, having some value or tendency to prove a matter of fact significant to the case.

residence. Place where one makes his/her home.

S

separate property. State laws vary, but generally, separate property is, has been, or can be controlled by the spouse owning it.

separation. Married persons living apart, either informally by one leaving the home or agreeing to "separate" while sharing a residence without sexual relations, or formally by obtaining a "legal separation" or negotiating a "separation agreement" setting out the terms of separate living.

separation agreement. Agreement between two married people who agree to live apart for an unspecified period of time, perhaps forever.

special master. Person appointed by the court to carry out an order of the court, such as selling property or mediating child custody cases.

spousal support. Payment for support of an ex-spouse (or a spouse while a divorce is pending) ordered by the court.

statute. Federal or state written law enacted by the Congress or state legislature, **respectively.**

T

tenancy by the entirety. Joint ownership of title by husband and wife, in which both have the right to the entire property, and, upon the death of one, the other has title (right of survivorship).

title. Ownership of real property or personal property, which stands against the right of anyone else to claim the property.

W

witness. 1) Person who testifies under oath in a trial (or a deposition which may be used in a trial if the witness is not available) with first-hand or expert evidence useful in a lawsuit; 2) a person who sees an event; 3) a person who observes the signing of a document like a will or a contract; or, 4) to sign a document verifying that he/she observed the execution of the document such as a will.

Y

your honor. Proper way to address a judge in court.

Appendix A: Resources

The following resources are agencies or written references that may deepen and further your understanding of issues related to the custody, support, and visitation topics set forth in this book. The listing is wide ranging and serves as a guide for further exploration in the field. The Statutes listed are helpful in gaining insight into the intent of the laws pertaining to custody, support, or visitation topics.

The Professional Academy of Custody Evaluators

Children's Rights Council

The National Center for Missing and Exploited Children. Includes information on the national Child Protection Act, the U.S. Department of Justice, Office of Juvenile Justice and Delinquency Prevention, and other resources.

Interstate Child Visitation Act

The Uniform Child Custody Jurisdiction Act of 1968 (UCCJA). Drafted to eliminate legal incentives for forum-shopping and child-snatching by parents.

Parental Kidnapping Prevention Act of 1980

Missing Children's Act of 1982

Missing Children's Assistance Act of 1984. Authorized the establishment of a national clearinghouse house (now The National Center for Missing and Exploited Children, to coordinate public and private efforts to locate, recover, or reunite missing children with their legal custodians and operate a national toll-free hotline through which individuals can report information on the location of missing children or request information on procedures for reuniting children with their legal custodians.

28 U.S.C. § 1738A- Full Faith and Credit Given to Child Custody Determinations

42 U.S.C. § 620 - Adoption Assistance and Child Welfare Act of 1980

42 U.S.C., Chapter 6 - The Children's Bureau

42 U.S.C., Chapter 7 - Social Security Act

Appendix B:
District Court
Administration

NOTE: *Pennsylvania has seven judicial districts that are each composed of two counties. They are:*

- Elk/Cameron
- Columbia/Montour*
- Warren/Forest
- Franklin/Fulton
- Perry/Juniata
- Snyder/Union
- Sullivan/Wyoming

*Each county has a District Court Administrator. The district number is listed in parentheses.

Adams County (51)
Adams County Courthouse
117 Baltimore Street
Gettysburg, PA 17325
717-337-9846

Allegheny County (5)
300 Frick Building
437 Grant Street
Pittsburgh, PA 15219
412-350-5410

Armstrong County (33)
Armstrong County Courthouse
Second Floor
Kittanning, PA 16201
724-548-3284

Beaver County (36)
Beaver County Courthouse
Third Street
Beaver, PA 15009
724-728-5700, Ext. 374

Bedford County (57)
Bedford County Courthouse
Annex #1
Bedford, PA 15522
814-623-4812

Berks County (23)
Berks County Services Center
633 Court Street
Reading, PA 19601
610-478-6208

Blair County (24)
Blair County Courthouse
423 Allegheny Street
Hollidaysburg, PA 16648
814-693-3050

Bradford County (42)
Bradford County Courthouse
301 Main Street
Towanda, PA 18848-1880
570-265-1707

Bucks County (7)
Bucks County Courthouse
55 East Court Street
Doylestown, PA 18901
215-348-6040

Butler County (50)
Butler County Courthouse
P.O. Box 1208
Butler, PA 16003
724-284-5298

Cambria County (47)
Cambria County Courthouse
200 South Center Street
Ebensburg, PA 15931
814-472-5440, Ext. 1552

Cameron/Elk Counties (59)
See Elk/Cameron Counties

Carbon County (56)
Carbon County Courthouse
P.O. Box 166
Jim Thorpe, PA 18229
570-325-8556

Centre County (49)
Centre County Courthouse
Room 208
Bellefonte, PA 16823
814-355-6727

Chester County (15)
Chester County Courthouse
Two North High Street
West Chester, PA 19380
610-344-6170

Clarion County (18)
Clarion County Courthouse
Main Street
Clarion, PA 16214
814-226-9351

Clearfield County (46)
Clearfield County Courthouse
230 East Market Street
Clearfield, PA 16830
814-765-2641, Ext. 32

Clinton County (25)
Clinton County Courthouse
230 East Water Street
Lock Haven, PA 17745
570-893-4016

Columbia County (26)
Columbia County Courthouse
P.O. Box 380
Bloomsburg, PA 17815
570-389-5667

Crawford County (30)
Crawford County Courthouse
903 Diamond Square
Meadville, PA 16335
814-333-7498

Cumberland County (9)
Cumberland County Courthouse
1 Courthouse Square
Carlisle, PA 17013
717-240-6200

Dauphin County (12)
Dauphin County Courthouse
Front & Market Streets
Harrisburg, PA 17101
717-257-1599

Delaware County (32)
Delaware County Courthouse
Media, PA 19063
610-891-4550

Elk/Cameron Counties (59)
Elk County Courthouse
P.O. Box 416
Ridgway, PA 15853
814-776-6144

Erie County (6)
Erie County Courthouse
140 West Sixth Street Room 201
Erie, PA 16501-1030
814-451-6295

Fayette County (14)
Fayette County Courthouse
61 East Main Street
Uniontown, PA 15401
724-430-1230

Forest/Warren Counties (37)
See Warren/Forest Counties

Franklin/Fulton Counties (39)
Franklin County Courthouse
157 Lincoln Way East
Chambersburg, PA 17201
717-261-3848

Greene County (13)
Greene County Courthouse
Waynesburg, PA 15370
724-852-5237

Huntingdon County (20)
Huntingdon County Courthouse
223 Penn Street
Huntingdon, PA 16652
814-643-5078

Indiana County (40)
Indiana County Courthouse
Fourth Floor
825 Philadelphia Street
Indiana, PA 15701
724-465-3955

Jefferson County (54)
Jefferson County Courthouse
200 Main Street
Brookville, PA 15825
814-849-1631

Juniata/Perry Counties (41)
See Perry/Juniata Counties

Lackawanna County (45)
Lackawanna County Courthouse
200 North Washington Avenue
Scranton, PA 18503
570-963-6773

Lancaster County (2)
Lancaster County Courthouse
50 North Duke Street
P.O. Box 83480
Lancaster, PA 17608-3480
717-299-8041

Lawrence County (53)
Lawrence County Government
Center
New Castle, PA 16101
724-656-1930

Lebanon County (52)
Lebanon County Courthouse
400 South Eighth Street
Room 308
Lebanon, PA 17042
717-274-2801, Ext. 375

Lehigh County (31)
Lehigh County Courthouse
455 West Hamilton Street
Allentown, PA 18105-1548
610-782-3014

Luzerne County (11)
Luzerne County Courthouse
200 North River Street
Wilkes-Barre, PA 18711
570-825-1593

Lycoming County (29)
Lycoming County Courthouse
48 West Third Street
Williamsport, PA 17701
570-327-2330

McKean County (48)
McKean County Courthouse
500 West Main Street
Smethport, PA 16749
814-887-3302

Mercer County (35)
Mercer County Courthouse
103 North Diamond Street
Mercer, PA 16137
412-662-3800, Ext. 2515

Mifflin County (58)
Mifflin County Courthouse
20 North Wayne Street
Lewistown, PA 17044
717-248-4613

Monroe County (43)
Monroe County Courthouse
Stroudsburg, PA 18360
570-517-3009

Montgomery County (38)
Montgomery County Courthouse
P.O. Box 311
Norristown, PA 19404
610-278-3228

Montour County (26)
Columbia County Courthouse
P.O. Box 380
Bloomsburg, PA 17815
570-389-5679

Northampton County (3)
Northampton County
Government Center
669 Washington Street
Easton, PA 18042
610-559-3042

Northumberland County (8)
Northumberland County
Courthouse
201 Market Street
Sunbury, PA 17801
570-988-4167

Perry/Juniata Counties (41)
Perry County Courthouse
P.O. Box 668
New Bloomfield, PA 17068
717-582-2131, Ext. 233

Philadelphia County (1)
336 City Hall
Philadelphia, PA 19107
215 686-2547

Pike County (60)
Pike County Courthouse
410 Broad Street
Milford, PA 18337
570-296-3556

Potter County (55)
Potter County Courthouse
Room 30
Coudersport, PA 16915
814-274-9720

Schuylkill County (21)
Schuylkill County Courthouse
401 North Second Street
Pottsville, PA 17901
570-628-1333

Snyder/Union Counties (17)
Snyder County Courthouse
P.O. Box 217
Middleburg, PA 17842
570-837-4238

Somerset County (16)
111 East Union Street
Suite 212
Somerset, PA 15501
814-445-1473

Sullivan/Wyoming Counties (44)
See Wyoming/Sullivan Counties

Susquehanna County (34)
Susquehanna County
Courthouse
P.O. Box 218
Montrose, PA 18801
570-278-4600, Ext. 195

Tioga County (4)
Tioga County Courthouse
118 Main Street
Wellsboro, PA 16901
570-724-9380

Union/Snyder Counties (17)
See Snyder/Union Counties

Venango County (28)
Venango County Courthouse
Liberty Street
Franklin, PA 16323
814-432-9606

Warren/Forest Counties (37)
Warren County Courthouse
204 Fourth Avenue
Warren, PA 16365
814-728-3530

Washington County (27)
Washington County Courthouse
1 South Main Street, Suite 2004
Washington, PA 15301
724-228-6797

Wayne County (22)
Wayne County Courthouse
925 Court Street
Honesdale, PA 18431
570-253-0101

Westmoreland County (10)
Westmoreland County
Courthouse
Main Street
Greensburg, PA 15601
724-830-3828

Wyoming/Sullivan Counties (44)
Wyoming County Courthouse
One Courthouse Square
Tunkhannock, PA 18657
570-836-3151

York County (19)
York County Courthouse
28 East Market Street
York, PA 17401
717-771-9234

Appendix C: Key Court Offices and Prothonotaries' Offices

Each of the Commonwealth's sixty-seven (67) counties has a Domestic Relations Section. You may locate the addresses of the Domestic Relations Section of the Common Pleas Court in your area by looking in the blue pages of your local telephone book.

Supreme Court

Eastern District	215-560-6370
Middle District	717-787-6181
Western District	412-565-2816

Superior Court 215-560-6800

Commonwealth Court 717-255-1600

County

Adams	717-337-9834
Allegheny	412-350-4200
Armstrong	724-548-3251
Beaver	724-728-5700
Bedford	814-623-4833
Berks	610-478-6970
Blair	814-693-3080
Bradford	570-265-1705
Bucks	215-348-6191
Butler	724-284-5220
Cambria	814-472-1638
Cameron	814-486-3355
Carbon	570-325-2481
Centre	814-355-6796
Chester	610-344-6300
Clarion	814-226-1119
Clearfield	814-765-2641
Clinton	570-893-4007
Columbia	570-389-5618
Crawford	814-333-7325
Cumberland	717-240-6195
Dauphin	717-255-2697
Delaware	610-891-4370
Elk	814-776-5343
Erie	814-451-6070
Fayette	724-430-1272
Forest	814-755-3526
Franklin	717-261-3858
Fulton	717-485-4212
Greene	724-852-5289
Huntingdon	814-643-1610
Indiana	724-465-3855

Jefferson	814-849-1625	Philadelphia	215-686-6652
Juniata	717-436-7715	Pike	570-296-7231
Lackawanna	570-963-6723	Potter	814-274-9740
Lancaster	717-299-8282	Schuylkill	570-628-1276
Lawrence	724-656-2143	Snyder	570-837-4202
Lebanon	717-228-4419	Somerset	814-445-1428
Lehigh	610-820-3148	Sullivan	570-946-7351
Luzerne	570-825-1743	Susquehanna	570-278-4600
Lycoming	570-327-2256	Tioga	570-724-9281
McKean	814-887-3270	Union	570-524-8751
Mercer	724-662-3800	Venango	814-432-9576
Mifflin	717-248-8146	Warren	814-728-3440
Monroe	570-420-3570	Washington	724-228-6770
Montgomery	610-278-3360	Wayne	570-253-5970
Montour	570-271-3010	Westmoreland	724-830-3500
Northampton	610-559-3060	Wyoming	570-836-3200
Northumberland	570-988-4151	York	717-771-9327
Perry	717-582-2131		

APPENDIX D: PENNSYLVANIA CONSOLIDATED STATUTES

DOMESTIC RELATIONS (TITLE 23)
SUPPORT, PROPERTY AND CONTRACTS.
CHAPTER 41 - GENERAL PROVISIONS

Sec. 4101. Liability for debts contracted before marriage.

Sec. 4102. Proceedings in case of debts contracted for necessaries.

Sec. 4103. (Reserved).

Sec. 4104. Right of married person to separate earnings.

Sec. 4105. Loans between married persons.

Sec. 4106. Construction of chapter.

Sec. 4101. Liability for debts contracted before marriage.

(a) **General rule.**—A spouse is not liable for the debts of the other spouse contracted before marriage.

(b) **Liability of property unaffected.**—This chapter does not protect the property of a married person from liability for debts contracted by or in the name of the married person by any person authorized to so contract.

Sec. 4102. Proceedings in case of debts contracted for necessaries.

In all cases where debts are contracted for necessaries by either spouse for the support and maintenance of the family, it shall be lawful for the creditor in this case to institute suit against the husband and wife for the price of such necessaries and, after obtaining a judgment, have an execution against the spouse contracting the debt alone; and, if no property of that spouse is found, execution may be levied upon and satisfied out of the separate property of the other spouse.

Sec. 4103. (Reserved).

Sec. 4104. Right of married person to separate earnings.

Except as otherwise provided in this title, the separate earnings of any married person of this Commonwealth, whether these earnings are wages for labor, salary, property, business or otherwise, shall accrue to and enure to the separate benefit and use of that married person independently of the other spouse, and so as not to be subject to any legal claim of the other spouse. However, in any action in which the ownership of such property is in dispute, the person claiming such property shall be compelled, in the first instance, to show title and ownership in the property.

Sec. 4105. Loans between married persons.

A married person may loan the other spouse money from the separate estate of the married person and take in security therefor a judgment or mortgage against the property of the other spouse which shall be valid as otherwise provided by law.

Sec. 4106. Construction of chapter.

This chapter shall not be construed to affect Part IV (relating to divorce).

DOMESTIC RELATIONS (TITLE 23)
SUPPORT, PROPERTY AND CONTRACTS.
CHAPTER 43 - SUPPORT MATTERS GENERALLY
SUBCHAPTER A— GENERAL PROVISIONS
SUBCHAPTER B— SUPPORT
SUBCHAPTER C— PROCEEDINGS GENERALLY
SUBCHAPTER D— PROCEEDINGS AGAINST
ENTIRETIES PROPERTY
SUBCHAPTER E— TITLE IV-D PROGRAM AND
RELATED MATTERS
SUBCHAPTER F— NEW HIRE REPORTING
SUBCHAPTER B — SUPPORT

Sec.4321. Liability for support.

Subject to the provisions of this chapter:

Married persons are liable for the support of each other according to their respective abilities to provide support as provided by law.

Parents are liable for the support of their children who are unemancipated and 18 years of age or younger.

Parents may be liable for the support of their children who are 18 years of age or older.

Sec.4322. Support guideline.

(a) **Statewide guideline.**—Child and spousal support shall be awarded pursuant to a Statewide guideline as established by general rule by the Supreme Court, so that persons similarly situated shall be treated similarly. The guideline shall be based upon the reasonable needs of the child or spouse seeking support and the ability of the obligor to provide support. In determining the reasonable needs of the child or spouse seeking support and the ability of the obligor to provide support, the guideline shall place primary emphasis on the net incomes and earning capacities of the parties, with allowable deviations for unusual needs, extraordinary expenses and other factors, such as the parties' assets, as warrant special attention. The guideline so developed shall be reviewed at least once every four years.

(b) **Rebuttable presumption.**—There shall be a rebuttable presumption, in any judicial or expedited process, that the amount of the award which would result from the application of such guideline is the correct amount of support to be awarded. A written finding or specific finding on the record that the application of the guideline would be unjust or inappropriate in a particular case shall be sufficient to rebut the presumption in that case, provided that the finding is based upon criteria established by the Supreme Court by general rule within one year of the effective date of this act.

Sec.4323. Support of emancipated child.

(a) **Emancipated child** —A court shall not order either or both parents to pay for the support of a child if the child is emancipated.

(b) **Marital status of parents immaterial** —In making an order for the support of a child, no distinction shall be made because of the marital status of the parents.

Sec.4324. Inclusion of spousal medical support.

In addition to periodic support payments, the court may require that an obligor pay a designated percentage of a spouse's reasonable and necessary health care expenses. If health care coverage is available through an obligor or obligee at no cost as a benefit of employment or at a reasonable

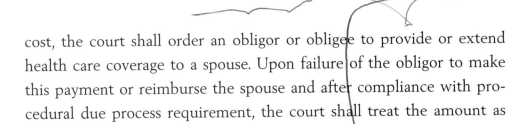

cost, the court shall order an obligor or obligee to provide or extend health care coverage to a spouse. Upon failure of the obligor to make this payment or reimburse the spouse and after compliance with procedural due process requirement, the court shall treat the amount as arrearages.

Sec.4325. Payment of order of support.

Unless procedures established by the department for the State disbursement unit provide otherwise, an order of support shall direct payment to be made payable to or payment to be made to the domestic relations section for transmission to the obligee or for transmission directly to a public body or public or private agency whenever the care, maintenance and assistance of the obligee is provided for by the public body or public or private agency.

Sec.4326. Mandatory inclusion of child medical support.

(a) **General rule** —In every proceeding to establish or modify an order which requires the payment of child support, the court shall ascertain the ability of each parent to provide health care coverage for the children of the parties, and the order shall provide health care coverage for each child as appropriate.

(b) **Noncustodial parent requirement** —If health care coverage is available at a reasonable cost to a noncustodial parent on an employment-related or other group basis, the court shall require that the noncustodial parent provide such coverage to the children of the parties. In cases where there are two noncustodial parents having such coverage available, the court shall require one or both parents to provide coverage.

(c) **Custodial parent requirement.**—If health care coverage is available at a reasonable cost to a custodial parent on an employment-related or other group basis, the court shall require that the custodial parent provide such coverage to the children of the parties, unless adequate health care coverage has already been provided through the noncustodial parent. In cases where the parents have shared custody of the child and coverage is available to both, the court shall require one or both parents to provide coverage, taking into account the financial ability of the parties and the extent of coverage available to each parent.

(d) Additional requirement —If the court finds that health care coverage is not available to either parent at a reasonable cost on an employment-related or other group basis, the court shall order either parent or both parents to obtain for the parties' children health insurance coverage which is available at reasonable cost.

(e) Uninsured expenses —The court shall determine the amount of any deductible and copayments which each parent shall pay. In addition, the court may require that either parent or both parents pay a designated percentage of the reasonable and necessary uncovered health care expenses of the parties' children, including birth-related expenses incurred prior to the filing of the complaint. Upon request of the domestic relations section, the department shall provide to the domestic relations section all birth-related expenses which the department has incurred in cases it has referred to the domestic relations section for child support services.

(f) Proof of insurance —Within 30 days after the entry of an order requiring a parent to provide health care coverage for a child or after any change in health care coverage due to a change in the parent's employment, the obligated parent shall submit to the other parent, or person having custody of the child, written proof that health care coverage has been obtained or that application for coverage has been made. Proof of coverage shall consist of at a minimum:

The name of the health care coverage provider.

Any applicable identification numbers.

Any cards evidencing coverage.

The address to which claims should be made.

A description of any restrictions on usage, such as prior approval for hospital admissions, and the manner of obtaining approval.

A copy of the benefit booklet or coverage contract.

A description of all deductibles and co-payments.

Five copies of any claim forms.

(g) Obligations of insurance companies —Every insurer doing business within this Commonwealth shall be obligated as follows:

(1) to permit the custodial parent or the provider, with the custodial parent's approval, to submit claims for covered services without the approval of the non-custodial parent and to make payment on such claims directly to such custodial parent, the provider or, in the case of Medical Assistance patients, to the department;

(2) to provide such information to the custodial parent as may be necessary to obtain benefits, including copies of benefit booklets, insurance contracts and claims information;

(3) if coverage is made available for dependents of the insured, to make such coverage available to the insured's children without regard to enrollment season restrictions, whether the child was born out of wedlock, whether the child is claimed as a dependent on the parent's Federal income tax return, whether the child resides in the insurer's service area, the amount of support contributed by a parent, the amount of time the child spends in the home or the custodial arrangements for the child;

(4) to permit the enrollment of children under court order upon application of the custodial parent, domestic relations section or the department within 30 days of receipt by the insurer of the order;

(4.1) not to disenroll or eliminate coverage of any child unless the insurer is provided satisfactory written evidence that a court order requiring coverage is no longer in effect or that the child is or will be enrolled in comparable health coverage through another insurer which will take effect no later than the effective date of such disenrollment;

(4.2) to receive, process and pay claims (whether or not on behalf of a child), including electronically submitted claims, submitted by the department within the time permitted by law without imposing any patient signature requirement or other requirement different from those imposed upon providers, agents or assignees of any insured individual;

(5) to provide the custodial parent who has complied with subsection (j) with the same notification of termination or modification of any health care coverage due to nonpayment of premiums or other reason as is provided to other insureds under the policy; and

(6) except as provided in paragraph (4.2), to not take into account the fact that any individual, whether or not a child, is eligible for or is being provided medical assistance when enrolling that individual or when making any payments for benefits to the individual or on the individual's behalf.

(h) Obligations of non-insurers —To the maximum extent permitted by Federal law, the obligations of subsection (g) shall apply to non-insurers providing health care coverage within this Commonwealth, including health maintenance organizations, self-insured employee health benefit plans and any other entity offering a service benefit plan.

(h.1) Obligations of employers —Every employer doing business within this Commonwealth shall be obligated as follows:

in any case in which a parent is required by a court order to provide health coverage for a child and the parent is eligible for family health coverage, the employer shall permit the insured parent to enroll any child who is otherwise eligible without regard to any enrollment season restrictions;

if the insured parent is enrolled but fails to make application to obtain coverage for such child, to enroll the child under the family coverage upon application by the child's other parent, the domestic relations section or the department; and not to disenroll or eliminate coverage of any such child unless the employer is provided satisfactory written evidence that the court or administrative order is no longer in effect, the child is or will be enrolled in comparable health coverage which will take effect not later than the effective date of such disenrollment or the employer has eliminated family health coverage for all of its employees.

(i) Obligations of custodial parent —The custodial parent shall comply with the insurer's existing claim procedures and present to the insurer one of the following documents:

a copy of a court order as defined in subsection (l); or

a release signed by the insured permitting the insurer to communicate directly with the custodial parent.

(j) Enforcement of order —The employee's share, if any, of premiums for health coverage shall be deducted by the employer and paid to the insurer or other entity providing health care coverage. If an obligated parent fails to comply with the order to provide health care coverage for a child, fails to pay medical expenses for a child or receives payment from a third party for the cost of medical services provided to such child and fails to reimburse the custodial parent or provider of services, the court shall:

If, after a hearing, the failure or refusal is determined to have been willful, impose the penalties of section 4345(a) (relating to contempt for noncompliance with support order).

Enter an order for a sum certain against the obligated parent for the cost of medical care for the child and for any premiums paid or provided for the child during any period in which the obligated parent failed or refused to provide coverage. Failure to comply with an order under this paragraph shall be subject to section 4348 (relating to attachment of income).

Upon failure of the obligated parent to make this payment or reimburse the custodial parent and after compliance with due process requirements, treat the amount as arrearages.

(k) Enforcement against insurers —Any insurer or other entity which violates the obligations imposed upon it under subsection (g) or (h) shall be civilly liable for damages and may be adjudicated in contempt and fined by the court.

(l) Definitions —As used in this section, the following words and phrases shall have the meanings given to them in this subsection:

"Birth-related expenses." Costs of reasonable and necessary health care for the mother or child or both incurred before, during or after the birth of a child both in or out of wedlock which are the result of the pregnancy or birth and which benefit either the mother or child. Charges not related to the pregnancy or birth shall be excluded.

"Child." A child to whom a duty of child support is owed.

"Health care coverage." Coverage for medical, dental, orthodontic, optical, psychological, psychiatric or other health care services for a child. For the purposes of this section, medical assistance under Sub-article (f) of Article IV of the act of June 13, 1967 (P.L.31, No.21), known as the Public Welfare Code, shall not be considered health care coverage.

"Insurer." A corporation or person incorporated or doing business in this Commonwealth by virtue of the act of May 17, 1921 (P.L.682, No.284), known as The Insurance Company Law of 1921; a hospital plan corporation as defined in 40 Pa.C.S. Ch. 61 (relating to hospital plan corporations); a professional health service plan corporation as defined in 40 Pa.C.S. Ch. 63 (relating to professional health services plan corporations); a beneficial society subject to 40 Pa.C.S. Ch. 65 (relating to fraternal benefit societies); a health maintenance organization; or any other person, association, partnership, common-law trust, joint stock company, nonprofit corporation, profit corporation or other entity conducting an insurance business.

"Medical child support order." An order which relates to the child's right to receive certain health care coverage and which:

> includes the name and last known mailing address of the parent providing health care coverage and the name and last known mailing address of the child;

> includes a reasonable description of the type of coverage to be provided or includes the manner in which coverage is to be determined;

> designates the time period to which the order applies;

> if coverage is provided through a group health plan, designates each plan to which the order applies; and

> includes the name and address of the custodial parent.

Sec.4327. Postsecondary educational costs.

(a) General rule —Where applicable under this section, a court may order either or both parents who are separated, divorced, unmarried or otherwise subject to an existing support obligation to provide equitably for educational costs of their child whether an application for this support is made before or after the child has reached 18 years of age. The responsibility to provide for postsecondary educational expenses is a shared responsibility between both parents. The duty of a parent to provide a postsecondary education for a child is not as exacting a requirement as the duty to provide food, clothing and shelter for a child of tender years unable to support himself. This authority shall extend to postsecondary education, including periods of undergraduate or vocational education after the child graduates from high school. An award for postsecondary educational costs may be entered only after the child or student has made reasonable efforts to apply for scholarships, grants and work-study assistance.

(b) Action to recover educational expenses.—An action to recover educational costs may be commenced:

by the student if over 18 years of age; or

by either parent on behalf of a child under 18 years of age, but, if the student is over 18 years of age, the student's written consent to the action must be secured.

(c) Calculation of educational costs —In making an award under this section, the court shall calculate educational costs as defined in this section.

(d) Grants and scholarships —The court shall deduct from the educational costs all grants and scholarships awarded to the student.

(e) Other relevant factors —After calculating educational costs and deducting grants and scholarships, the court may order either parent or both parents to pay all or part of the remaining educational costs of their child. The court shall consider all relevant factors which appear reasonable, equitable and necessary, including the following:

The financial resources of both parents.

The financial resources of the student.

The receipt of educational loans and other financial assistance by the student.

The ability, willingness and desire of the student to pursue and complete the course of study.

Any willful estrangement between parent and student caused by the student after attaining majority.

The ability of the student to contribute to the student's expenses through gainful employment. The student's history of employment is material under this paragraph.

Any other relevant factors.

(f) When liability may not be found —A court shall not order support for educational costs if any of the following circumstances exist:

Undue financial hardship would result to the parent.

The educational costs would be a contribution for postcollege graduate educational costs.

The order would extend support for the student beyond the student's twenty-third birthday. If exceptional circumstances exist, the court may order educational support for the student beyond the student's twenty-third birthday.

(g) Parent's obligation —A parent's obligation to contribute toward the educational costs of a student shall not include payments to the other parent for the student's living expenses at home unless the student resides at home with the other parent and commutes to school.

(h) Termination or modification of orders —Any party may request modification or termination of an order entered under this section upon proof of change in educational status of the student, a material change in the financial status of any party or other relevant factors.

(i) Applicability — This act shall apply to all divorce decrees, support agreements, support orders, agreed or stipulated court orders, property settlement agreements, equitable distribution agreements, custody agreements and/or court orders and agreed to or stipulated court orders in effect on, executed or entered since, November 12, 1992.

In addition, this act shall apply to all pending actions for support. This section shall not supersede or modify the express terms of a voluntary written marital settlement agreement or any court order entered pursuant thereto.

(j) Definitions —As used in this section, the following words and phrases shall have the meanings given to them in this subsection:

"**Educational costs.**" Tuition, fees, books, room, board and other educational materials.

"Postsecondary education." An educational or vocational program provided at a college, university or other postsecondary vocational, secretarial, business or technical school.

DOMESTIC RELATIONS (TITLE 23)
CHILDREN AND MINORS
CHAPTER 51 - GENERAL PROVISIONS

Sec. 5101. Attainment of full age.

Sec. 5102. Children declared to be legitimate.

Sec. 5103. Acknowledgment and claim of paternity.

Sec. 5104. Blood tests to determine paternity.

Sec. 5101. Attainment of full age.

(a) **Age for entering into contracts** —Any individual 18 years of age and older shall have the right to enter into binding and legally enforceable contracts and the defense of minority shall not be available to such individuals.

(b) **Age for suing and being sued** —Except where otherwise provided or prescribed by law, an individual 18 years of age and older shall be deemed an adult and may sue and be sued as such.

Sec. 5102. Children declared to be legitimate.

(a) **General rule** —All children shall be legitimate irrespective of the marital status of their parents, and, in every case where children are born out of wedlock, they shall enjoy all the rights and privileges as if they had been born during the wedlock of their parents except as otherwise provided in Title 20 (relating to decedents, estates and fiduciaries).

(b) **Determination of paternity** —For purposes of prescribing benefits to children born out of wedlock by, from and through the father, paternity shall be determined by any one of the following ways:

If the parents of a child born out of wedlock have married each other.

If, during the lifetime of the child, it is determined by clear and convincing evidence that the father openly holds out the child to be his and either receives the child into his home or provides support for the child.

If there is clear and convincing evidence that the man was the father of the child, which may include a prior court determination of paternity.

Sec. 5103. Acknowledgment and claim of paternity.

(a) Acknowledgment of paternity —The father of a child born to an unmarried woman may file with the Department of Public Welfare, on forms prescribed by subsection (c), an acknowledgment of paternity of the child which shall include the consent of the mother of the child, supported by her affidavit. In such case, the father shall have all the rights and duties as to the child which he would have had if he had been married to the mother at the time of the birth of the child, and the child shall have all the rights and duties as to the father which the child would have had if the father had been married to the mother at the time of birth.

(b) Claim of paternity —If the mother of the child fails or refuses to join in the acknowledgment of paternity provided for in subsection (a), the Department of Public Welfare shall index it as a claim of paternity. The filing and indexing of a claim of paternity shall not confer upon the putative father any rights as to the child except that the putative father shall be entitled to notice of any proceeding brought to terminate any parental rights as to the child.

(c) Duty of hospital or birthing center —Upon the birth of a child to an unmarried woman, an agent of the hospital or birthing center where the birth occurred shall:

Provide the newborn's birth parents with an opportunity to complete an affidavit acknowledging paternity. The completed, signed and notarized affidavit shall be sent to the Department of Public Welfare. A copy shall be given to each of the birth parents. This affidavit shall contain:

> (i) A sworn, signed statement by the birth mother consenting to the assertion of paternity.
>
> (ii) A signed, notarized statement by the birth father acknowledging his paternity.
>
> (iii) A written explanation of the parental duties and parental rights which arise from signing such a statement.
>
> (iv) The Social Security numbers and addresses of both birth parents.

Provide written information, furnished by the Department of Public Welfare to the birth mother, which explains the benefits of having the child's paternity established, the availability of paternity establishment services and the availability of child support enforcement agencies.

(d) Conclusive evidence —An acknowledgment of paternity shall constitute conclusive evidence of paternity in any action to establish support. An acknowledgment of paternity may be set aside by the court only upon clear and convincing evidence that the defendant was unaware of the fact that he was acknowledging paternity when the acknowledgment was signed.

(e) Transfer —The Department of Health shall transfer to the Department of Public Welfare all acknowledgments or claims of paternity filed with the Department of Health under prior statutes.

(f) Certifications —The Department of Public Welfare shall provide necessary certifications under Part III (relating to adoption) as to whether any acknowledgment or claim of paternity has been filed in regard to any child who is a prospective adoptive child.

Sec. 5104. Blood tests to determine paternity.

(a) Short title of section —This section shall be known and may be cited as the Uniform Act on Blood Tests to Determine Paternity.

(b) Scope of section —

Civil matters —This section shall apply to all civil matters.

Criminal proceedings —This section shall apply to all criminal proceedings subject to the following limitations and provisions:

(i) An order for the tests shall be made only upon application of a party or on the initiative of the court.

(ii) The compensation of the experts shall be paid by the party requesting the blood test or by the county, as the court shall direct.

(iii) The court may direct a verdict of acquittal upon the conclusions of all the experts under subsection (f). Otherwise, the case shall be submitted for determination upon all the evidence.

(iv) The refusal of a defendant to submit to the tests may not be used in evidence against the defendant.

(c) Authority for test —In any matter subject to this section in which paternity, parentage or identity of a child is a relevant fact, the court, upon its own initiative or upon suggestion made by or on behalf of any person whose blood is involved, may or, upon motion of any party to the action made at a time so as not to delay the proceedings unduly, shall order the mother, child and alleged father to submit to blood tests. If any party refuses to submit to the tests, the court may resolve the question of paternity, parentage or identity of a child against the party or enforce its order if the rights of others and the interests of justice so require.

(d) Selection of experts —The tests shall be made by experts qualified as examiners of blood types, who shall be appointed by the court. The experts shall be called by the court as witnesses to testify to their findings and shall be subject to cross-examination by the parties. Any party or person at whose suggestion the tests have been ordered may demand that other experts qualified as examiners of blood types perform independent tests under order of court, the results of which may be offered in evidence. The number and qualifications of experts shall be determined by the court.

(e) Compensation of experts —The compensation of each expert witness appointed by the court shall be fixed at a reasonable amount. It shall be paid as the court shall order. Subject to general rules, the court may order that it be paid by the parties in such proportions and at such times as it shall prescribe or that the proportion of any party be paid by the county and that, after payment by the parties or the county, or both, all or part or none of it be taxed as costs in the action. Subject to general rules, the fee of an expert witness called by a party but not appointed by the court shall be paid by the party calling him, but shall not be taxed as costs in the action.

(f) Effect of test results —If the court finds that the conclusions of all the experts as disclosed by the evidence based upon the tests are that the alleged father is not the father of the child, the question of paternity, parentage or identity of a child shall be resolved accordingly. If the experts disagree in their findings or conclusions, the question shall be submitted upon all the evidence.

(g) Effect on presumption of legitimacy —The presumption of legitimacy of a child born during wedlock is overcome if the court finds that the conclusions of all the experts as disclosed by the evidence based upon the tests show that the husband is not the father of the child.

CHILDREN AND MINORS.
CHAPTER 53. CUSTODY
SUBCHAPTER A - GENERAL PROVISIONS

SUBCHAPTER B - CHILD CUSTODY JURISDICTION

Appendix E: Child Custody Jurisdiction Act and Parental Kidnapping Prevention Act

Sec. 75-a. Short title. This article shall be known as the "Uniform Child Custody Jurisdiction Act."

Sec. 75-b. Purposes of article; construction of provisions.

1. The general purposes of this article are to:

    (a) avoid jurisdictional competition and conflict with courts of other states in matters of child custody which have in the past resulted in the shifting of children from state to state with harmful effects on their well-being;

    (b) promote cooperation with the courts of other states to the end that a custody decree is rendered in that state which can best decide the case in the interest of the child;

    (c) assure that litigation concerning the custody of a child take place ordinarily in the state with which the child and his family have the closest connection and where significant evidence concerning his care, protection, training, and personal relationships is most readily available, and that courts of this state decline the exercise of jurisdiction when the child and his family have a closer connection with another state;

(d) discourage continuing controversies over child custody in the interest of greater stability of home environment and of secure family relationships for the child;

(e) deter abductions and other unilateral removals of children undertaken to obtain custody awards;

(f) avoid re-litigation of custody decisions of other states in this state insofar as feasible;

(g) facilitate the enforcement of custody decrees of other states;

(h) promote and expand the exchange of information and other forms of mutual assistance between the courts of this state and those of other states concerned with the same child; and

(i) make uniform the law of those states which enact it.

2. This article shall be construed to promote the general purposes stated in this section.

Sec. 75-c. Definitions. As used in this article, the following terms have the following meanings:

1. **"Contestant"** means a person, including a parent, who claims a right to custody or visitation rights with respect to a child.

2. **"Custody determination"** means a court decision and court orders and instructions providing for the temporary or permanent custody of a child, including visitation rights.

3. **"Custody proceeding"** includes proceedings in which a custody determination is at issue or is one of several issues including any action or proceeding brought to annul a marriage or to declare the nullity of a void marriage, or for a separation, or for a divorce, but not including proceedings for adoption, child protective proceedings or proceedings for permanent termination of parental custody, or proceedings involving the guardianship and custody of neglected or dependent children, or proceedings initiated pursuant to section three hundred fifty-eight-a of the social services law.

4. **"Decree" or "custody decree"** means a custody determination contained in a judicial decree or order made in a custody proceeding, and includes an initial decree and a modification decree.

5. **"Home state"** means the state in which the child at the time of the commencement of the custody proceeding, has resided with his parents, a parent, or a person acting as parent, for at least six consecutive months. In the case of a child less than six months old at the time of the commencement of the proceeding, home state means the state in which the child has resided with any of such persons for a majority of the time since birth.

6. **"Initial decree"** means the first custody decree concerning a particular child.

7. **"Modification decree"** means a custody decree which modifies or replaces a prior decree, whether made by the court which rendered the prior decree or by another court.

8. **"Physical custody"** means actual possession and control of a child.

9. **"Person acting as parent"** means a person, other than a parent, who has physical custody of a child and who has either been awarded custody by a court or claims a right to custody.

10. **"State"** means any state, territory, or possession of the United States, the Commonwealth of Puerto Rico, and the District of Columbia.

Sec. 75-d. Jurisdiction to make child custody determinations.

1. A court of this state which is competent to decide child custody matters has jurisdiction to make a child custody determination by initial or modification decree only when:

(a) this state (i) is the home state of the child at the time of commencement of the custody proceeding, or (ii) had been the child's home state within six months before commencement of such proceeding and the child is absent from this state because of his removal or retention by a person claiming his custody or for other reasons, and a parent or person acting as parent continues to live in this state; or

(b) it is in the best interest of the child that a court of this state assume jurisdiction because (i) the child and his parents, or the child and at least one contestant, have a significant connection with this state, and (ii) there is within the jurisdiction of the court substantial evidence concerning the child's present or future care, protection, training, and personal relationships; or

(c) the child is physically present in this state and (i) the child has been abandoned or (ii) it is necessary in an emergency to protect the child; or

(d) (i) it appears that no other state would have jurisdiction under prerequisites substantially in accordance with paragraph (a), (b), or (c), or another state has declined to exercise jurisdiction on the ground that this state is the more appropriate forum to determine the custody of the child, and (ii) it is in the best interest of the child that this court assume jurisdiction.

2. Except under paragraphs (c) and (d) of subdivision one of this section, physical presence in this state of the child, or of the child and one of the contestants, is not alone sufficient to confer jurisdiction on a court of this state to make a child custody determination.

3. Physical presence of the child, while desirable, is not a prerequisite for jurisdiction to determine his custody.

Sec. 75-e. Notice and opportunity to be heard. Before making a decree under this article, reasonable notice and opportunity to be heard shall be given to the contestants, any parent whose parental rights have not been previously terminated, and any person who has physical custody of the child. If any of these persons is outside the state, notice and opportunity to be heard shall be given pursuant to section seventy-five-f of this article. Any person who is given notice and an opportunity to be heard pursuant to this section shall be deemed a party to the proceeding for all purposes under this article.

Sec. 75-f. Notice to persons outside the state.

1. If a person cannot be personally served with notice within the state, the court shall require that such person be served in a manner reasonably calculated to give actual notice, as follows:

(a) by personal delivery outside the state in the manner prescribed in section three hundred thirteen of the civil practice law and rules;

(b) by any form of mail addressed to the person and requesting a receipt; or

(c) in such manner as the court, upon motion, directs, including publication, if service is impracticable under paragraph (a) or (b) of subdivision one of this section.

2. Notice under this section shall be served, mailed, delivered, or last published at least twenty days before any hearing in this state.

3. Proof of service outside the state shall be by affidavit of the individual who made the service, or in the manner prescribed by the order pursuant to which the service is made. If service is made by mail, proof may be a receipt signed by the addressee or other evidence of delivery to the addressee.

4. Notice is not required if a person submits to the jurisdiction of the court.

Sec. 75-g. Simultaneous proceedings in other states.

1. A court of this state shall not exercise its jurisdiction under this article if at the time of filing the petition a proceeding concerning the custody of the child was pending in a court of another state exercising jurisdiction substantially in conformity with this article, unless the proceeding is stayed by the court of the other state because this state is a more appropriate forum or for other reasons.

2. Before hearing the petition in a custody proceeding the court shall examine the pleadings and other information supplied by the parties under section seventy-five-j of this article. If the court has reason to believe that proceedings may be pending in another state it shall direct an inquiry to the state court administrator or other appropriate official of the other state.

3. If the court is informed during the course of the proceeding that a proceeding concerning the custody of the child was pending in another state before the court assumed jurisdiction it shall stay the proceeding and communicate with the court in which the other proceeding is pending to the end that the issue may be litigated in the more appropriate forum and that information be exchanged in accordance with sections seventy-five-s through seventy-five-v of this article. If a court of this state has made a custody decree before being informed of a pending proceeding in a court of another state, it shall immediately inform that court of the fact. If the court is informed that a proceeding was commenced in another state after it assumed jurisdiction, it shall likewise inform the other court to the end that the issues may be litigated in the more appropriate forum.

Sec. 75-h. Inconvenient forum.

1. A court which has jurisdiction under this article to make an initial or modification decree may decline to exercise its jurisdiction any time before making a decree if it finds that it is an inconvenient forum to make a custody determination under the circumstances of the case and that a court of another state is a more appropriate forum.

2. A finding of inconvenient forum may be made upon the court's own motion or upon motion of a party or a guardian ad litem or other representative of the child.

3. In determining if it is an inconvenient forum, the court shall consider if it is in the interest of the child that another state assume jurisdiction. For this purpose it may take into account the following factors, among others, whether:

(a) another state is or recently was the child's home state;

(b) another state has a closer connection with the child and his family or with the child and one or more of the contestants;

(c) substantial evidence concerning the child's present or future care, protection, training, and personal relationships is more readily available in another state;

(d)the parties have agreed on another forum which is no less appropriate; and

(e)the exercise of jurisdiction by a court of this state would contravene any of the purposes stated in section seventy-five-b of this article.

1. Before determining whether to decline or retain jurisdiction the court may communicate with a court of another state and exchange information pertinent to the assumption of jurisdiction by either court with a view to assuring that jurisdiction will be exercised by the more appropriate court and that a forum will be available to the parties.

2. If the court finds that it is an inconvenient forum and that a court of another state is a more appropriate forum, it may dismiss the proceedings, or it may stay the proceedings upon condition that a custody proceeding be promptly commenced in another named state or upon any other conditions which may be just and proper, including the condition that a moving party stipulate his consent and submission to the jurisdiction of the other forum.

3. Where the court has jurisdiction of an action or proceeding brought to annul a marriage or to declare the nullity of a void marriage or for a separation or for a divorce, the court may decline to exercise jurisdiction of an application for a custody determination made therein while retaining jurisdiction of the matrimonial action.

4. If it appears to the court that it is clearly an inappropriate forum it may require the party who commenced the proceedings to pay, in addi-

tion to the costs of the proceedings in this state, necessary travel and other expenses, including attorneys` fees, incurred by other parties or their witnesses. Payment shall be made to the clerk of the court for remittance to the proper party.

5. Upon dismissal or stay of proceedings under this section the court shall inform the court found to be the more appropriate forum of such dismissal or stay, or if the court which would have jurisdiction in the other state is not certainly known, shall transmit the information to the court administrator or other appropriate official for forwarding to the appropriate court.

6. Any communication received from another state to the effect that its courts have made a finding of inconvenient forum because a court of this state is the more appropriate forum shall be filed with the clerk of the appropriate court. Upon assuming jurisdiction the court of this state shall inform the original court of this fact.

Sec. 75-i. Jurisdiction declined because of conduct.

1. If the petitioner for an initial decree has wrongfully taken the child from another state or has engaged in similar reprehensible conduct the court may decline to exercise jurisdiction if this is just and proper under the circumstances.

2. Unless required in the interest of the child, the court shall not exercise its jurisdiction to modify a custody decree of another state if the petitioner, without consent of the person entitled to custody, has improperly removed the child from the physical custody of the person entitled to custody or has improperly retained the child after a visit or other temporary relinquishment of physical custody. If the petitioner has violated any other provision of a custody decree of another state the court may decline to exercise its jurisdiction if this is just and proper under the circumstances.

3. In appropriate cases a court dismissing a petition under this section may charge the petitioner with necessary travel and other expenses, including attorneys` fees, incurred by other parties or their witnesses.

Sec. 75-j. Pleadings and affidavits; duty to inform court.

1. Except as provided in subdivisions four and five of this section, every party to a custody proceeding shall, in his or her first pleading or in an affidavit attached to that pleading, give information under oath as to the child's present address, the places where the child has lived within the last five years, and the names and present addresses of the persons with whom the child has lived during that period. In this pleading or affidavit every party shall further declare under oath whether he or she:

(a) has participated as a party, witness, or in any other capacity in any other litigation concerning the custody of the same child in this or any other state;

(b) has information of any custody proceeding concerning the child pending in a court of this or any other state; and

(c) knows of any person not a party to the proceedings who has physical custody of the child or claims to have custody or visitation rights with respect to the child.

2. If the declaration as to any of the above items is in the affirmative the declarant shall give additional information under oath as required by the court. The court may examine the parties under oath as to details of the information furnished and as to other matters pertinent to the court's jurisdiction and the disposition of the case.

3. If, during the pendency of a custody proceeding, any party learns of another custody proceeding concerning the child in this or another state, he shall immediately inform the court of this fact.

4. In an action for divorce or separation, or to annul a marriage or declare the nullity of a void marriage,

(a) where neither party is in default in appearance or pleading and the issue of custody is uncontested, the affidavit required by this section need not be submitted. In any other such action, such affidavit shall be submitted by the parties within twenty days after joinder of issue on the question of custody, or at the time application for a default judgment is made.

(b) Notwithstanding any other provision of law, if the party seeking custody of the child has resided or resides in a residential program for victims of domestic violence as defined in subdivision four of section four hundred fifty-nine-a of the social services law, the present address of the child and the present address of the party seeking custody and the address of the residential program for victims of domestic violence shall not be revealed.

(c) Notwithstanding any other provision of law, the court shall waive disclosure of the present and all prior addresses of the child or a party upon notice to the adverse party when such relief is necessary for the physical or emotional safety of a child or a party.

5. Notwithstanding any other provision of law, in any custody proceeding, the court shall waive disclosure of the present or a prior address of the child or a party when such relief is necessary for the physical or emotional safety of a child or a party. Application for an order waiving disclosure of the present or a prior address of the child or a party shall be on notice to all other parties, who shall have an opportunity to be heard. Provided, however, that in no case shall the address of a residential program for victims of domestic violence, as defined in subdivision four of section four hundred fifty-nine-a of the social services law, be disclosed.

Sec. 75-k. Additional parties. If the court learns from information furnished by the parties pursuant to section seventy-five-j of this article, or from other sources that a person not a party to the custody proceeding has physical custody of the child or claims to have custody or visitation rights with respect to the child, it shall order that person to be joined as a party and to be duly notified of the pendency of the proceeding and of his joinder as a party. If the person joined as a party is outside this state he shall be served with process or otherwise notified in accordance with section seventy-five-f of this article.

Sec. 75-l. Appearance of parties and the child.

1. The court may order any party to the proceeding who is in the state to appear personally before the court. If that party has physical custody of the child the court may order that he appear personally with the child.

2. If a party to the proceeding whose presence is desired by the court is outside the state with or without the child the court may order that the notice given under section seventy-five-f of this article include a statement directing that party to appear personally with or without the child and declaring that failure to appear may result in a decision adverse to that party.

3. If a party to the proceeding who is outside the state is directed to appear under subdivision two or desires to appear personally before the court with or without the child, the court may require another party to pay to the clerk of the court travel and other necessary expenses of the party so appearing and of the child if this is just and proper under the circumstances.

Sec. 75-m. Force and effect of custody decrees. A custody decree rendered by a court of this state which had jurisdiction under section seventy-five-d of this article shall be binding upon all parties who have been personally served in this state or notified pursuant to section seventy-five-f of this article or who have submitted to the jurisdiction of the court, and who have been given an opportunity to be heard. As to these parties the custody decree is conclusive as to all issues of law and fact decided and as to the custody determination made unless and until that determination is modified pursuant to law, including the provisions of this article.

Sec. 75-n. Recognition of out-of-state custody decrees. The courts of this state shall recognize and enforce an initial or modification decree of a court of another state which had assumed jurisdiction under statutory provisions substantially in accordance with this article or which was made under factual circumstances meeting the jurisdictional standards of this article, so long as the decree has not been modified in accordance with jurisdictional standards substantially similar to those of this article.

Sec. 75-o. Modification of custody decree of another state.

1. If a court of another state has made a custody decree, a court of this state shall not modify that decree unless (1) it appears to the court of this state that the court which rendered the decree does not now have jurisdiction under jurisdictional prerequisites substantially in accordance with this article or has declined to assume jurisdiction to modify the decree and (2) the court of this state has jurisdiction.

2. If a court of this state is authorized under subdivision one of this section and section seventy-five-i of this article to modify a custody decree of another state, it shall give due consideration to the transcript of the record and other documents of all previous proceedings submitted to it in accordance with section seventy-five-v of this article.

Sec. 75-p. Filing and enforcement of custody decree of another state.

1. A certified copy of a custody decree of another state may be filed in the office of the clerk of the supreme court or of the family court. The clerk shall treat the decree in the same manner as a custody decree of the supreme court or of the family court. A custody decree so filed has the same effect and shall be enforced in like manner as a custody decree rendered by a court of this state.

2. A person violating a custody decree of another state which makes it necessary to enforce the decree in this state may be required to pay necessary travel and other expenses, including attorneys` fees, incurred by the party entitled to the custody or his witnesses.

Sec. 75-q. Certified copies of custody decrees. The clerk of the supreme court or the family court, at the request of the court of another state or, upon payment of the appropriate fees, if any, at the request of a party to the custody proceeding, the attorney for a party or a representative of the child shall certify and forward a copy of the decree to that court or person.

Sec. 75-r. Examination of witnesses outside the state. In addition to other procedural devices available to a party, any party to the proceeding or a guardian ad litem or other representative of the child may examine witnesses, including parties and the child, in another state by deposition or otherwise in accordance with the applicable provisions of the civil practice law and rules.

Sec. 75-s. Hearings and studies in another state; orders to appear.

1. A court of this state may request the appropriate court of another state to hold a hearing to adduce evidence, to order a party within its jurisdiction, to produce or give evidence under other procedures of that state, or to have social studies made with respect to the custody of a child involved in proceedings pending in the court of this state; and to forward to the court of this state certified copies of the transcript of the record of the hearing, the evidence otherwise adduced, or any social studies prepared in compliance with the request. The cost of the services may be assessed against the parties.

2. A court of this state may request the appropriate court of another state to order a party to custody proceedings pending in the court of this state to appear in the proceedings, and if that party has physical custody of the child, to appear with the child. The request may state that travel and other necessary expenses of the party and of the child whose appearance is desired will be assessed against another party or will otherwise be paid.

Sec. 75-t. Assistance to courts of other states.

1. Upon request of the court of another state the courts of this state which are competent to hear custody matters may order a party or witness in this state to appear at an examination to be conducted in the same manner as if such person were a party to or witness in an action pending in the supreme court. A certified copy of the deposition or the evidence otherwise adduced shall be forwarded by the clerk of the court to the court which requested it.

2. A person within the state may voluntarily give his testimony or statement for use in a custody proceeding outside this state.

3. Upon request of the court of another state a competent court of this state may order a person within the state to appear alone or with the child in a custody proceeding in another state. The court may condition compliance with the request upon assurance by the other state that travel and other necessary expenses will be advanced or reimbursed.

Sec. 75-u. Preservation of evidence for use in other states. In any custody proceeding in this state the court shall preserve the pleadings, orders and decrees, any record that has been made of its hearings, social studies, and other pertinent documents until the child reaches twenty-one years of age. Upon appropriate request of the court of another state the court shall forward to the other court certified copies of any or all of such documents.

Sec. 75-v. Request for court records from another state. If a custody decree has been rendered in another state concerning a child involved in a custody proceeding pending in a court of this state, the court of this state upon taking jurisdiction of the case shall request of the court of the other state a certified copy of the transcript of any court record and other documents mentioned in section seventy-five-u.

Sec. 75-w. International application. The general policies of this article extend to the international area. The provisions of this article relating to the recognition and enforcement of custody decrees of other states apply to custody decrees and decrees involving legal institutions similar in nature to custody institutions rendered by appropriate authorities of other nations if reasonable notice and opportunity to be heard were given to all affected persons.

Sec. 75-x. Priority. Upon the request of a party to a custody proceeding which raises a question of existence or exercise of jurisdiction under this article the case shall be given calendar priority and handled expeditiously.

Sec. 75-y. Separability. If any part of this article or the application thereof to any person or circumstance is adjudged invalid by a court of competent jurisdiction, such judgment shall not affect or impair the validity of the remainder of such article or the application thereof to other persons and circumstances.

Sec. 75-z. Inconsistent provisions of other laws superseded. Insofar as the provisions of this article are inconsistent with the provisions of any other law, general, special or local, the provisions of this article shall be controlling.

Parental Kidnapping Prevention Act (PKPA)
28 USCS § 1738A (2002)

Sec. 1738A. Full faith and credit given to child custody determinations

(a) The appropriate authorities of every State shall enforce according to its terms, and shall not modify except as provided in subsections (f), (g), and (h) of this section, any custody determination or visitation determination made consistently with the provisions of this section by a court of another State.

(b) As used in this section, the term—
    (1) "child" means a person under the age of eighteen;
    (2) "contestant" means a person, including a parent or grandparent, who claims a right to custody or visitation of a child;
    (3) "custody determination" means a judgment, decree, or other order of a court providing for the custody of a child, and includes permanent and temporary orders, and initial orders and modifications;
    (4) "home State" means the State in which, immediately preceding the time involved, the child lived with his parents, a parent, or a person acting as parent, for at least six consecutive months, and in the case of a child less than six months old, the State in which the child lived from birth with any of such persons. Periods of temporary absence of any of such persons are counted as part of the six-month or other period;
    (5) "modification" and "modify" refer to a custody or visitation determination which modifies, replaces, supersedes, or

otherwise is made subsequent to, a prior custody or visitation determination concerning the same child, whether made by the same court or not;

(6) "person acting as a parent" means a person, other than a parent, who has physical custody of a child and who has either been awarded custody by a court or claims a right to custody;

(7) "physical custody" means actual possession and control of a child;

(8) "State" means a State of the United States, the District of Columbia, the Commonwealth of Puerto Rico, or a territory or possession of the United States; and

(9) "visitation determination" means a judgment, decree, or other order of a court providing for the visitation of a child and includes permanent and temporary orders and initial orders and modifications.

(c) A child custody or visitation determination made by a court of a State is consistent with the provisions of this section only if—

(1) such court has jurisdiction under the law of such State; and

(2) one of the following conditions is met:

(A) such State (i) is the home State of the child on the date of the commencement of the proceeding, or (ii) had been the child's home State within six months before the date of the commencement of the proceeding and the child is absent from such State because of his removal or retention by a contestant or for other reasons, and a contestant continues to live in such State;

(B) (i) it appears that no other State would have jurisdiction under subparagraph (A), and (ii) it is in the best interest of the child that a court of such State assume jurisdiction because (I) the child and his parents, or the child and at least one contestant, have a significant connection with such State other than mere physical presence in such State, and (II) there is available in such State substantial evidence concerning the child's present or future care, protection, training, and personal relationships;

(C) the child is physically present in such State and (i) the child has been abandoned, or (ii) it is necessary in an emergency to protect the child because the child, a sibling, or parent of the child has been subjected to or threatened with mistreatment or abuse;

(D) (i) it appears that no other State would have jurisdiction under subparagraph (A), (B), (C), or (E), or another State has declined to exercise jurisdiction on the ground that the State whose jurisdiction is in issue is the more appropriate forum to determine the custody or visitation of the child, and (ii) it is in the best interest of the child that such court assume jurisdiction; or

(E) the court has continuing jurisdiction pursuant to subsection (d) of this section.

(d) The jurisdiction of a court of a State which has made a child custody or visitation determination consistently with the provisions of this section continues as long as the requirement of subsection (c)(1) of this section continues to be met and such State remains the residence of the child or of any contestant.

(e) Before a child custody or visitation determination is made, reasonable notice and opportunity to be heard shall be given to the contestants, any parent whose parental rights have not been previously terminated and any person who has physical custody of a child.

(f) A court of a State may modify a determination of the custody of the same child made by a court of another State, if—

(1) it has jurisdiction to make such a child custody determination; and

(2) the court of the other State no longer has jurisdiction, or it has declined to exercise such jurisdiction to modify such determination.

(g) A court of a State shall not exercise jurisdiction in any proceeding for a custody or visitation determination commenced during the pendency of a proceeding in a court of another State where such court of that other State is exercising jurisdiction consistently with the provisions of this section to make a custody determination.

(h) A court of a State may not modify a visitation determination made by a court of another State unless the court of the other State no longer has jurisdiction to modify such determination or has declined to exercise jurisdiction to modify such determination.

APPENDIX F:
SUPPORT GUIDELINES

This appendix contains the support guideline computation owrksheet and chart. See Chapter 10 for a full explanation of child support calculations. This worksheet and chart, however, will assist you in figuring out your own support payments on form 3 in Appendix G. Check with an attorney or the court to ensure that you have filled in your own calculations accurately.

SUPPORT GUIDELINE COMPUTATIONS
CHILD SUPPORT

		DEFENDANT	PLAINTIFF
1.	Total Gross per Period	8,000.00	6,000.00
2.	Net Income	6,000.00	4,000.00
3.	Conversion to Monthly Amount	1,000.00	700.00
4.	COMBINE OF BOTH DEFENDANT AND PLAINTIFF	17,000.00	
5.	Proportionate Expenditure (determined from chart)	x .20%	
6.	Basic Child Support (multiply #4 by #5)	340.00	
7.	Additional support if required		
8.	Total Support	340.00	
9.	Percentage of each parent's obligation (divide line #3 by #4)	58%	41%
10.	Each parent's obligation	$197.00	$139.40

SPOUSAL SUPPORT WITH DEPENDENT CHILDREN

11.	DEFENDANT'S MONTHLY NET INCOME	$1,000.00
12.	LESS PLAINTIFF'S MONTHLY NET INCOME	$700.00
13.	DIFFERENCE	$300.00
14.	LESS DEFENDANT'S CHILD SUPPORT OBLIGATION	$197.00
15.	DIFFERENCE	$103.00
16.	MULTIPLY BY 30%	x .30
17.	AMOUNT OF MONTHLY SPOUSAL SUPPORT	$30.90
18.	COMBINE SPOUSAL SUPPORT (LINE 17) AND CHILD SUPPORT FOR A TOTAL SUPPORT AWARD	$227.90

SPOUSAL SUPPORT WITHOUT DEPENDENT CHILDREN

19.	DEFENDANT'S MONTHLY NET INCOME (LINE 3)	$_____
20.	LESS PLAINTIFF'S MONTHLY INCOME (LINE 3)	$_____
21.	DIFFERENCE	$_____
22.	MULTIPLY BY 40%	x .40
23.	AMOUNT OF MONTHLY SPOUSAL SUPPORT	$_____

CHART OF PROPORTIONAL EXPENDITURES

The chart of proportional expenditures is as follows:

PROPORTION OF <u>NET MONTHLY INCOME</u> ON CHILDREN BY INCOME LEVEL

<u>Income Levels</u>

<u>Children</u>	$500- $700	$701- $995	$996- $1,143	$1,144- $1,291	$1,292- $1,439
1	23.5	23.0	22.5	22.0	21.5
2	36.5	35.8	35.1	34.4	33.7
3	45.7	44.8	43.9	43.0	42.1
4 or more	50.0	49.0	48.1	47.2	46.3
	$1,440- $1,587	$1,588- $1,735	$1,736- $1,883	$1,884- $2,031	$2,032- $2,179
1	21.0	20.5	20.0	19.5	19.0
2	33.0	32.3	31.6	30.9	30.2
3	41.2	40.3	39.4	38.5	37.6
4 or more	45.4	44.5	43.6	42.7	41.8
	$2,180- $2,327	$2,328- $2,475	$2,476- $2,623	$2,624- $2,771	$2,772- $2,919
1	18.5	18.0	17.5	17.0	16.5
2	29.5	28.8	28.1	27.4	26.7
3	36.7	35.8	34.9	34.0	33.1
4 or more	40.9	40.0	39.1	38.2	37.3
	$2,920- $3,067	$3,068- $3,215	$3,216- $3,363	$3,364- $4,000	$4,001- $5,000
1	16.0	15.5	15.0	14.5	14.0
2	26.0	25.3	24.6	23.9	23.2
3	32.2	31.3	30.4	29.5	28.6
4 or more	36.4	35.5	34.6	33.7	32.8
	$5, 001- $6,000	$6,001- $7,000	$7,001- $8,000	$8,001- $9,000	$9,001- $10,000
1	13.5	13.0	12.5	12.0	11.5
2	22.5	221.8	21.1	20.4	19.7
3	27.7	26.8	25.9	25.0	24.1
4 or more	31.9	31.0	30.1	29.2	28.3

The circled value 20.0 is indicated by an arrow in the row for 1 child, $1,736-$1,883 income level.

⟶ This is the number used in the computation on page 194, line 5.

Appendix G: Forms

Table of Forms

_____ (IN THE COURT OF COMMON PLEAS OF

PLAINTIFF, (

(_____COUNTY, PENNSYLVANIA

v. (

(CIVIL DIVISION

(

_____ (NO:

DEFENDANT.

NOTICE TO DEFEND AND CLAIM RIGHTS

YOU HAVE BEEN SUED IN COURT. IF YOU WISH TO DEFEND AGAINST THE CLAIM SET FORTH IN THE FOLLOWING PAGES, YOU MUST TAKE PROMPT ACTION. YOU ARE WARNED THAT IF YOU FAIL TO DO SO, THE CASE MAY PROCEED WITHOUT YOU AND A DECREE OF DIVORCE OR ANNULMENT MAY BE ENTERED AGAINST YOU BY THE COURT. A JUDGMENT MAY ALSO BE ENTERED AGAINST YOU FOR ANY OTHER CLAIM OR RELIEF REQUESTED IN THESE PAPERS BY THE PLAINTIFF. YOU MAY LOSE MONEY OR PROPERTY OR OTHER RIGHTS IMPORTANT TO YOU, INCLUDING CUSTODY OR VISITATION OF YOUR CHILD(REN).

WHEN THE GROUND FOR THE DIVORCE ARE INDIGNITIES OR IRRETRIEVABLE BREAKDOWN OF THE MARRIAGE, YOU MAY REQUEST MARRIAGE COUNSELING. A LIST OF MARRIAGE COUNSELORS IS AVAILABLE IN THE OFFICE OF THE PROTHONOTARY AT _____ _____, PENNSYLVANIA.

IF YOU DO NOT FILE A CLAIM FOR ALIMONY, DIVISION OF PROPERTY, LAWYERS FEES, OR EXPENSES BEFORE A DIVORCE OR ANNULMENT IS GRANTED, YOU MAY LOSE THE RIGHT TO CLAIM ANY OF THEM

YOU SHOULD TAKE THIS PAPER TO YOUR LAWYER AT ONCE. IF YOU DO NOT HAVE A LAWYER OR CANNOT AFFORD ONE, GO TO OR TELEPHONE THE OFFICE SET FORTH BELOW TO FIND OUT WHERE YOU CAN GET LEGAL HELP.

LAWYERS REFERRAL SERVICE

_____

_____

Telephone: _____

_____

For Petitioner

Address: _____

_____

Telephone: _____

REQUIRED INFORMATION   TODAY'S DATE _____

Plaintiff/Defendant

_____ **County Domestic Relations Department**

Income and Expense Statement

Name _____

Date of Birth _____ SS# _____ Phone # _____

Home Address _____

Drivers License # _____

Employer _____ Position _____

Address _____

Phone _____ Date Employed _____

Other Employment _____

Health Insurance Company Name _____ Policy # _____

Address_____ Group # _____

1. Check Method of Payment and List Gross Income:

   Paid: ☐ Every 2 weeks   ☐ Twice Monthly   ☐ Monthly   ☐ Weekly $_____

                                                                         Gross Income

2. Subtract tax deductions:

   Federal Income Tax $ _____
   Social Security   _____
   State Income Tax   _____
   Local Income Tax   _____

   Health Insurance   _____
   Union Dues   _____
   Pension Contributions   _____
   Credit Union   _____
   Other Deductions   _____

   Total Deductions   _____   -$_____

                        Subtract Totals from Gross Income

                                                             _____
                                                             NET INCOME

ALL OTHER INCOME

List any interest and dividends, pensions and annuity, Social Security, net income from property, Unemployment Compensation, Workmen's Compensation or other, such as royalties, expense accounts, gifts, etc. (if no other income check none)   NONE ☐

_____ $ _____

_____   _____

_____   _____

Total Other Income   _____
Deduct Estimated Income Taxes on such Other Income _____
Final Net Income Per Week $ _____

_____ COUNTY

D.R.S.

Docket _____   Date _____

Defendant _____   C.O. _____

Plaintiff _____

Rule 1910.16-3 Support Guidelines Formula

    (a) The formula for the determination of the amount of support is as follows:

SUPPORT GUIDELINE COMPUTATIONS
CHILD SUPPORT

		DEFENDANT	PLAINTIFF	
1.	Total Gross Income Per Pay Period	_____	_____	
2.	Net Income	_____	_____	
3.	Conversion to Monthly Amount	_____	_____	
4.	COMBINE INCOME OF BOTH DEFENDANT AND PLAINTIFF		_____	
5.	Proportionate Expenditure (determined from chart)		x _____	%
6.	Basic Child Support (multiply #4 by #5)		= _____	
7.	Additional support if required		_____	
8.	Total Support		_____	
9.	Percentage of each parent's obligation (divide line #3 by #4)	_____ %	_____ %	
10.	Each parent's obligation	$ _____	$ _____	

SPOUSAL SUPPORT WITH DEPENDENT CHILDREN

11.	DEFENDANT'S MONTHLY NET INCOME	$ _____	
12.	LESS PLAINTIFF'S MONTHLY NET INCOME	- $ _____	
13.	DIFFERENCE	$ _____	
14.	LESS DEFENDANT'S CHILD SUPPORT OBLIGATION	- $ _____	
15	DIFFERENCE	$ _____	
16.	MULTIPLY BY 30%	_____ .30	
17.	AMOUNT OF MONTHLY SPOUSAL SUPPORT	$ _____	

18.   COMBINE SPOUSAL SUPPORT (line 17) AND CHILD SUPPORT FOR A TOTAL SUPPORT AWARD.

SPOUSAL SUPPORT WITHOUT DEPENDENT CHILDREN

19.	DEFENDANT'S MONTHLY NET INCOME (line #3)	$ _____	
20.	LESS PLAINTIFF'S MONTHLY INCOME (line #3)	- $ _____	
21.	DIFFERENCE	$ _____	
22.	MULTIPLY BY 40%	x _____ .40	
23.	AMOUNT OF MONTHLY SPOUSAL SUPPORT	$ _____	

RULE 1910.16-3 DRS 10/92

_____   (IN THE COURT OF COMMON PLEAS OF

              PLAINTIFF,   (

                        (_____COUNTY, PENNSYLVANIA

        v.   (

                        (CIVIL DIVISION

                        (

_____   (NO:

             DEFENDANT.

CERTIFICATE (Proof) OF SERVICE

    PLAINTIFF NAME: _____ of the Commonwealth of Pennsylvania, hereby affirms the following statement under penalty of perjury:

    1.   I am the plaintiff in this action. I hereby certify that on _____, 200___ (DATE), I caused a copy of the attached:

    NAME OF DOCUMENT: _____

to be served upon

Defendant's NAME: _____

ADDRESS: _____

by depositing a true copy of same enclosed in a post-paid properly addressed wrapper, in a depository under the exclusive care and custody of the U.S. Postal Service within the Commonwealth of Pennsylvania.

Dated: _____

                        _____

                        NAME: _____,

                                    Plaintiff.

_____ COUNTY COURT OF COMMON PLEAS

CIVIL COVER SHEET

Docket No. _____

I (a) PLAINTIFFS   **DEFENDANTS**

(b) PLAINTIFF'S ATTORNEYS (ADDRESS)   **DEFENDANT'S ATTORNEY'S (IF KNOWN) (ADDRESS)**

II. <u>MANDATORY ARBITRATION</u>
Does this fall under the mandatory arbitration
requirements per Local Rule 1301?

Yes or No

III. <u>ALTERNATE DISPUTE RESOLUTION REQUESTED</u>
_____ Summary Jury Trial
_____ Other: See "Guide to Alternate Dispute
Resolution Programs" Published by the
_____County Bar Association

IV. <u>CAUSE(S) OF ACTION</u> (Cite the statutes or rules of law under which you are filing and write a brief statement of causes(s).)

V. <u>GENERAL NATURE OF SUIT</u> (Place an X in <u>one area only</u> that most accurately describes your case)

<u>CONTRACT</u>
_____ Insurance
_____ PA Bond
_____ Collection Suits
_____ Construction
_____ Other - List in
      IV above

<u>REAL PROPERTY</u>
_____ Condemnation
_____ Foreclosure
_____ Landlord & Tenant
_____ Partition
_____ Mechanics' Lien
_____ Environment
_____ Other - List
      in IV above
_____ Address of Property _____

<u>PERSONAL INJURY</u>
_____ Motor Vehicle
_____ Product Liability
_____ Medical Malpractice
_____ Other Prof. Liability
_____ Intentional
_____ Premises
_____ Other - List in
      IV above

<u>PRISONER PETITIONS</u>
_____ Habeas Corpus
_____ Mandamus
_____ Other - List in
      IV above

_____ <u>LABOR</u>

<u>DOMESTIC RELATIONS</u>
_____ Divorce
_____ Protection from Abuse
_____ Custody/Visitation
_____ Other - List in IV above
_____ Support

<u>OTHER STATUTES</u>
_____ Zoning Appeal
_____ School Board Appeal
_____ License Suspension Appeal
_____ Assessment Appeal
_____ Other - List in IV above

_____ <u>TAX LIEN &</u>
         <u>TAX MATTERS</u>
<u>OTHER</u>
_____ List in IV above

      (a) Is this an equity case? Yes or No   (b) Does it involve a governmental body? Yes or No

VI. <u>ORIGIN</u> (Mark only 1)
___ 1 Original   ___ 2 Removed from   ___ 3 Confessed   ___ 4 Transferred   ___ 5 Appeal   ___ 6 Appeal to   ___ 7 Foreign
     Complaint   Federal Court   Judgments by   From Another   From   Court from   Judgment
     of Writ   Complaint   District or   Govt.   District
                                      or Praecipe   County (specify)   Agency   Justice
                                                                        Judgment

VII. <u>REQUESTED IN COMPLAINT</u>

      (a) Is this a CLASS ACTION YES or NO

      (c) Amount demanded in complaint _____

      (b) Circle YES only if jury demanded in complaint:
             JURY DEMAND: YES or NO
             Will you accept 6 jurors?   YES or NO

VIII. <u>RELATED CASE(S) IF ANY</u>   JUDGE _____   DOCKET NUMBER _____

      Case Caption

_____
DATE

_____
SIGNATURE OF FILING PARTY OR ATTORNEY OF RECORD

IN THE COURT OF COMMON PLEAS
OF _____ COUNTY, PENNSYLVANIA

	:	**CIVIL DIVISION**
_____	:	
Plaintiff	:	No.
	:	
vs.	:	TEMPORARY CUSTODY PETITION
	:	
_____	:	Filed on Behalf of Plaintiff
Defendant	:	
	:	Plaintiff Name and
	:	_____
	:	_____
	:	_____
	:	Phone ( ) _____

PETITION FOR (TEMPORARY) CUSTODY

AND NOW, comes the petitioner, _____, pro se, and respectfully represents in support of petitioner's complaint that:

1. The petitioner, _____, is an adult individual residing at _____, _____, Pennsylvania _____. This is petitioner's petition for custody.

2. The respondent, _____, is an adult individual residing at _____, _____, Pennsylvania _____.

3. The parties were married on _____/_____/_____, separated on _____/_____/_____.

4. The petitioner seeks custody of the following children, not born out of wedlock:

   Child One, DOB; _____/_____/_____;   Child Two, DOB: _____/_____/_____;

   Child Three, DOB; _____/_____/_____;   Child Four, DOB: _____/_____/_____;

5. The children are presently in the physical custody of _____.

6. State and medical conditions of the children:

7. During the past _____ years, the children have resided with the following persons and at the following addresses:

☐ The children has/have resided with their natural parents all their lives in Pennsylvania.

☐ Other:

8. The natural mother of children is _____, residing at the address above-listed.

9. The natural father of the children is _____, residing at the address above-listed.

10. The Court has jurisdiction to determine the custody of the children because Pennsylvania is the children's home state as defined by PS Section 5344. The children and the parties have significant connection with the Commonwealth and substantial evidence concerning the present and future care, protection, training, and personal relationships of the children exists in Pennsylvania.

11. Petitioner has no information of a custody proceeding concerning the children pending in any court of this Commonwealth or any other State.

12. Petitioner does not know of a person not a party to this proceeding who has physical custody of the children or claims to have custody or visitation rights with respect to the children.

13. The best interests and permanent welfare of the children will be served by granting the relief requested herein because of the attachment of the children to their mother/father and/or the special needs of (child).

14. This matter has not been heard by a custody counselor in the past.

15. Each parent whose physical rights to the children has not been terminated and the persons who have physical custody of the children have been named as parties to this action. All of the persons known to have a claim of right to custody or visitation of the children will be given notice of the pendency of this action and the right to intervene.

16. Petitioner has been advised of the requirement to attend the seminar entitled "Children Coping With Divorce."

WHEREFORE, petitioner respectfully requests this Court to grant:

1. Temporary Emergency Custody to Petitioner;

2. Order that the children be retained by or returned immediately to:

Pennsylvania / mother / father.

3. Custody and primary residency of the children to the petitioner.

Respectfully submitted,

_____
NAME

IN THE COURT OF COMMON PLEAS

OF _____ COUNTY, PENNSYLVANIA

	:	CIVIL DIVISION
	:	
Plaintiff	:	No.
	:	
vs.	:	
	:	
Defendant	:	

VERIFICATION

I, _____, depose and say that the facts set forth in the foregoing document are true and correct to the best of my knowledge, information, and belief. This is made subject to the penalties of the 18 Pa. C.S.A. Section 4904 relating to unsworn falsification to authorities.

_____

Date: _____

IN THE COURT OF COMMON PLEAS

OF _____ COUNTY, PENNSYLVANIA

	:	CIVIL DIVISION
	:	
Plaintiff	:	No.
	:	
vs.	:	
	:	
Defendant	:	

ORDER OF COURT

AND NOW, this the _____ day of _____, 200_____, it is hereby DECREED and ORDERED that the Plaintiff, _____, is AWARDED TEMPORARY CUSTODY of parties _____ minor children

_____

and it is further ORDERED that the Children be immediately returned to the CUSTODY AND CONTROL of Plaintiff pending the proceedings scheduled before the Custody _____ and further Order of this Court.

By the Court:

_____

JUDGE

IN THE COURT OF COMMON PLEAS OF _____ COUNTY, PENNSYLVANIA

_____,
          Plaintiff,

                             Case No. _____

V.

                             Division; _____

_____,
          Defendant

NOTICE OF HEARING

TO: spouse name and address

     Please be advised that a Hearing on the following matter:_____ has been scheduled on the _____ day of _____, 20___, in Courtroom _____ of the _____ County Courthouse, (insert address of Courthouse) before the Honorable _____.

_____
(Insert Plaintiff's Name)

Domestic Relations Information Sheet

DATE	CASE I.D. NO.

INFORMATION ON PARENTS

FATHER OF CHILDREN *(First Name)*   *(Middle Initial)*   *(Last Name)*   ALIAS, IF ANY

MAILING ADDRESS	RESIDENTIAL ADDRESS, IF DIFFERENT FROM MAILING ADDRESS

DATE OF BIRTH	SOCIAL SECURITY NO	DPW NO

HEIGHT	WEIGHT	RACE	HAIR	EYES	DISTINGUISHING FEATURES

PLACE OF EMPLOYMENT	MEDICAL INSURANCE CARRIER NAME, ADDRESS

HOME PHONE NO.	WORK PHONE NO.	POLICY NO.	CHILDREN COVERED? ☐ Yes ☐ No

OCCUPATION	ATTORNEY'S NAME AND ADDRESS

SALARY $_____ per _____	ATTORNEY I.D. NO.

MOTHER OF CHILDREN *(First Name)*   *(Middle Initial)*   *(Last Name)*   ALIAS, IF ANY

MAILING ADDRESS	RESIDENTIAL ADDRESS, IF DIFFERENT FROM MAILING ADDRESS

DATE OF BIRTH	SOCIAL SECURITY NO	DPW NO

HEIGHT	WEIGHT	RACE	HAIR	EYES	DISTINGUISHING FEATURES

PLACE OF EMPLOYMENT	MEDICAL INSURANCE CARRIER NAME, ADDRESS

HOME PHONE NO.	WORK PHONE NO.	POLICY NO.	CHILDREN COVERED? ☐ Yes ☐ No

OCCUPATION	ATTORNEY'S NAME AND ADDRESS

SALARY $_____ per _____	ATTORNEY I.D. NO.

RECEIVING ASSISTANCE? ☐ Yes ☐ No	DPW NO.	DISTRICT RECEIVING FROM	SEMI-MONTHLY GRANT AMOUNT	TOTAL NO. OF PEOPLE IN HOUSEHOLD
PARTIES EVER MARRIED? ☐ Yes ☐ No	MARRIAGE DATE	PLACE	DATE OF SEPARATION DATE OF DIVORCE	PLACE

MATERNAL GRANDMOTHER'S MAIDEN NAME	MATERNAL GRANDFATHER'S NAME

09-788

217

INFORMATION ON CARETAKER OF CHILD(REN) OTHER THAN PARENTS (IF ANY)

NAME _(First)_ _(Middle Initial)_ _(Last)_	RELATIONSHIP	DATE OF BIRTH

ADDRESS	HOME PHONE NO.	WORK PHONE NO.
	SOCIAL SECURITY NO.	

INFORMATION ON CHILDREN

NAME _(First)_ _(Middle Initial)_ _(Last)_	SEX	DATE OF BIRTH
	☐ Male ☐ Female	

SOCIAL SECURITY NO.	PLACE OF BIRTH	ACTIVE ON CASH ASSISTANCE? ☐ Yes ☐ No

FATHER LISTED ON BIRTH CERTIFICATE? ☐ Yes ☐ No	BORN OUT OF WEDLOCK? ☐ Yes ☐ No	WAS PATERNITY ESTABLISHED? ☐ Yes ☐ No	DATE OF PATERNITY ESTABLISHMENT

NAME _(First)_ _(Middle Initial)_ _(Last)_	SEX	DATE OF BIRTH
	☐ Male ☐ Female	

SOCIAL SECURITY NO.	PLACE OF BIRTH	ACTIVE ON CASH ASSISTANCE? ☐ Yes ☐ No

FATHER LISTED ON BIRTH CERTIFICATE? ☐ Yes ☐ No	BORN OUT OF WEDLOCK? ☐ Yes ☐ No	WAS PATERNITY ESTABLISHED? ☐ Yes ☐ No	DATE OF PATERNITY ESTABLISHMENT

NAME _(First)_ _(Middle Initial)_ _(Last)_	SEX	DATE OF BIRTH
	☐ Male ☐ Female	

SOCIAL SECURITY NO.	PLACE OF BIRTH	ACTIVE ON CASH ASSISTANCE? ☐ Yes ☐ No

FATHER LISTED ON BIRTH CERTIFICATE? ☐ Yes ☐ No	BORN OUT OF WEDLOCK? ☐ Yes ☐ No	WAS PATERNITY ESTABLISHED? ☐ Yes ☐ No	DATE OF PATERNITY ESTABLISHMENT

NAME _(First)_ _(Middle Initial)_ _(Last)_	SEX	DATE OF BIRTH
	☐ Male ☐ Female	

SOCIAL SECURITY NO.	PLACE OF BIRTH	ACTIVE ON CASH ASSISTANCE? ☐ Yes ☐ No

FATHER LISTED ON BIRTH CERTIFICATE? ☐ Yes ☐ No	BORN OUT OF WEDLOCK? ☐ Yes ☐ No	WAS PATERNITY ESTABLISHED? ☐ Yes ☐ No	DATE OF PATERNITY ESTABLISHMENT

NAME _(First)_ _(Middle Initial)_ _(Last)_	SEX	DATE OF BIRTH
	☐ Male ☐ Female	

SOCIAL SECURITY NO.	PLACE OF BIRTH	ACTIVE ON CASH ASSISTANCE? ☐ Yes ☐ No

FATHER LISTED ON BIRTH CERTIFICATE? ☐ Yes ☐ No	BORN OUT OF WEDLOCK? ☐ Yes ☐ No	WAS PATERNITY ESTABLISHED? ☐ Yes ☐ No	DATE OF PATERNITY ESTABLISHMENT

09-788 (Reverse)

Plaintiff(s)

COURT OF COMMON PLEAS
FAMILY DIVISION

TERM.

vs.

Defendant(s)   No.

NOTICE TO DEFEND AND CLAIM RIGHTS	ADVERTENCIA SOBRE COMO DEFENDERSE Y RECLAMAR DERECHOS

You have been sued in court for

☐ Divorce   ☐ Annulment of Marriage
☐ Support   ☐ Custody and Visitation
☐ Division of Property   ☐ Alimony
☐ Temporary Alimony   ☐ Attorney Fees
☐ Costs

You have been sued in court for

☐ Divorcio   ☐ Annulacion de Matrimonia
☐ Pension Alimenticia   ☐ Custodia y Visitacion
  (Mantenimiento)
☐ Division de Propiedad   ☐ Pension Alimenticia
☐ Pension Alimenticia   ☐ Costas de Abogado
  Temporana   ☐ Costas

You have been sued in court. If you wish to defend against the claims set forth in the following pages, you must take prompt action. You are warned that if you fail to do so, the case may proceed without you and a decree of divorce or annulment may be entered against you by the court. A judgment may also be entered against you for any other claim of relief requested in these papers by the plaintiff. You may lose money or property or other rights important to you, including custody or visitation of your children.

When the ground for the divorce is indignities or irretrievable breakdown of the marriage, you may request marriage counseling. A list of marriage counselors is available in the Office of the Prothonotary at Room 286 City Hall, Philadelphia, PA 19107.

IF YOU DO NOT FILE A CLAIM FOR ALIMONY, DIVISION OF PROPERTY, LAWYER'S FEES OR EXPENSES BEFORE A DIVORCE OR ANNULMENT IS GRANTED, YOU MAY LOSE THE RIGHT TO CLAIM ANY OF THEM.
YOU SHOULD TAKE THIS PAPER TO YOUR LAWYER AT ONCE. IF YOU DO NOT HAVE A LAWYER OR CANNOT AFFORD ONE, GO TO OR TELEPHONE THE OFFICE SET FORTH BELOW TO FIND OUT WHERE YOU CAN GET LEGAL HELP.

```
Lawyer Reference Service
    One Reading Center
Philadelphia, Pennsylvania    19107
    Telephone:  238-1701
```

Usted ha sido demandado en corte. Si usted desea defender el reclamo puesto en contra suya en las siguientes paginas, tiene que tomar accion inmediatamente. Se le advierta que si falla en hacerlo, el casa puede ser procasado sin su de usted por la corte. Un juicio tambien puede ser registrado en contra de usted por la corte. Un jucio tambien puede ser registrado en su contra por cualquier otro reclamo o peticion requerida en ostos papeles por el querellante. Usted puede perder dinero, propiedad o otros derechos importantes para usted, incluyendo custodia o visitacion para sus ninos.

Cuando la causa del divorcio es maltrato o trastorno irrearable en el matrimonio, usted debe solicitar consejeria matrimonial. Una lista de consejeros matrimoniales esta disponible en las oficinas del pro-thonotario en Cuarto 286 de la Alcadia, Filadelfia, PA 19107 (Room 286 City Hall, Philadelphia, PA 19107.

SI USTED NO REGISTRA UN RECLAMADO PARA LA PENCION ALIMENTICIA, LA REPARTICION DE PROPIEDADES, EL HONORARIO DEL ABOGADO O GASTOS ANTES DE QUE EL UN DIVORCIO O ANNULACION SEA OTORGADO, USTED PUEDE PERDER EL DERECHO DE RECLAMAR CULAQUIERA DE ESTOS.
USTED DEBE LLEVAR ESTE PAPEL A SU ABOGADO INMEDIATAMENTE. SI USTED NO TIENE UN ABOGADO O NO PUEDE PAGAR POR LOS SERVICIOS DE UNO, VAYA O LLAME A LA OFICINA INDICADA, PARA AVERIGUAR DONDE PUEDE OBTENER ASISTENCIA LEGAL.

```
SERVICIO DE REFERENCIA DE ABOGADO
        Uno Reading Centro
    Filadelfia, Pennsylvania    19107
        Telefono:  238-1701
```

Former Domestic Relations Proceeding ☐ *Yes* ☐ *No*
If child support is claimed, is such child or children receiving Public Assistance ☐ *Yes* ☐ *No*

Domestic Relations No.

Complaint In Divorce

<u>COUNT I - Divorce</u>

Plaintiff, by (his/her) attorney(s)   *, respectfully represents:*

1. Plaintiff is   *, who currently resides at*
                    (Name)   *(Address)*
in the City of   *, County of*   *, Pennsylvania, since*
                                                                                (Date)

2. Defendant is   *, who currently resides at*
                    (Name)   *(Address)*
            in the City of   *, County of*   *, Pennsylvania, since*

3. Plaintiff and defendant are sui juris, and both have been bona fide residents of the Commonwealth of Pennsylvania for a period of more than six (6) months immediately preceding the filing of this Complaint. (If only one is a resident of the Commonwealth of Pennsylvania for the required time, so state.)

4. The parties were married on the   day of   ,   , at
State of   A certified copy (the original) of the marriage certificate is attached hereto, made a part hereof and marked Exhibit "A." (Explanation if unavailable)

5. (State cause of action and section(s) of Divorce Code under which plaintiff is proceeding.)

6. There have been no prior actions of divorce or for annulment between the parties except

7. The parties have/have not entered into a written agreement as to (support, visitation of children, alimony, and property division.) (A true and correct copy of said agreement is attached hereto, made a part hereof and marked Exhibit "B.")

WHEREFORE, plaintiff requests your Honorable Court to enter a decree in divorce, divorcing plaintiff and defendant. (In the event it is desired that the agreement be made part of the Court Order, add: "and the agreement attached hereto as Exhibit "B" be incorporated in the decree and entered as an order of this Court.")

<u>COUNT II - Equitable Distribution</u>

8. Paragraphs 1 through 4 of this Complaint are incorporated herein by reference as though set forth in full .

9. Plaintiff and defendant have acquired property, both real and personal during their marriage from
until   , the date of their separation.

10. Plaintiff and defendant have been unable to agree as to an equitable division of said property.

WHEREFORE, plaintiff requests your Honorable Court to equitably divide all marital property.

<u>COUNT III - Alimony</u>

11. Paragraphs 1 through 4 of this Complaint are incorporated herein by reference as though set forth in full.

12. Plaintiff lacks sufficient property to provide for (his/her) reasonable means and is unable to support (himself/herself)   through appropriate employment.

13. Plaintiff requires reasonable support to adequately maintain (himself/herself) in accordance with the standard of living established during the marriage.

WHEREFORE, plaintiff requests your Honorable Court to enter an award of alimony.

COUNT IV - Support for Children

14. Paragraphs 1 through 4 of this Complaint are incorporated herein by reference as though set forth in full .

15. Plaintiff and defendant are parents of   unemancipated children:

Name(s)   Age   Sex   Date of Birth   Residence

16. Support is sought for (Names of children)

17. Plaintiff is (is not) on Public Assistance and receives $ per   for wife and/or children.

18. Defendant earns in excess of $ (net/gross) per year and has assets in excess of $

19. Defendant has failed to provide for adequate and reasonable support for said children in accordance with the standard of living of the parties.   or   (Defendant has been paying $ per   for support of said children and plaintiff desires said payments be continued by Order of the Court.

WHEREFORE, plaintiff requests an award of reasonable and adequate support for the children of the parties.

COUNT V - Alimony Pendente Lite, Counsel Fees, Costs and Expenses

20. Paragraphs 1 through 4 and 18 of this Complaint are incorporated herein by reference as though set forth in full .

21. Plaintiff has employed counsel, but is unable to pay the necessary and reasonable attorney's fees for said counsel.

22. Plaintiff is unable to sustain herself/himself during the course of this litigation.

WHEREFORE, plaintiff requests your Honorable Court to enter an award of Alimony Pendente lite, interim counsel fees, costs and expenses, until final hearing and thereupon award such additional counsel fees, costs and expenses as deemed appropriate.

COUNT VI - Custody
Partial Custody and/or Visitation

23. Paragraphs 1 through 4 and 15 of this Complaint are incorporated herein by reference as though set forth in full .

24. In the past five years, the parties' children have resided (addresses where the children have resided and the name and present address of the parties with whom they have resided.)

25. Plaintiff has/has not participated (as a party, witness, or in any other capacity) in any other litigation concerning the custody of the same child/children in this or any other State. (Note: if this averment is in the affirmative, plaintiff shall explain such participation and the status or disposition of such case.)

26. Plaintiff has/has no information of any custody proceeding concerning the child/children pending in this or any other case. *(Note: if this averment is in the affirmative, plaintiff shall supply all available information concerning such proceeding.)*

27. Plaintiff knows/does not know of any person not a party to the proceedings who has physical custody of the child/children or who claims to have custody or visitation rights with respect to the child/children. *(Note: If this averment is in the affirmative, plaintiff shall supply all available information concerning such person/persons.)*

28. The best interest of the child(ren) would be served by granting requested relief.

WHEREFORE, plaintiff prays your Honorable Court to grant custody   partial custody   visitation right to plaintiff.

BY: _____

Attorneys for Plaintiff

VERIFICATION TO COMPLAINT IN DIVORCE

Plaintiff verifies that the statements made in this complaint are true and correct. Plaintiff understands that false statements   herein are made subject to the penalties of 18 Pa. C.S. Section 4904, relating to unsworn falsification to authorities.

_____

PLAINTIFF

_____

ATTORNEY FOR PLAINTIFF

_____

DATE

COMMONWEALTH OF PENNSYLVANIA
COUNTY OF PHILADELPHIA

COUNSELING NOTICE UNDER PA. R.C.P. RULE 1920.45(a) (1)

COURT OF COMMON PLEAS
Family Court Division

vs.

_____ Term, 20_____

No. _____

COUNSELING NOTICE

The Divorce Code of Pennsylvania requires that you be notified of the availability of counseling where a divorce is sought under any of the following grounds:

Section   3301(a)   (6)   Indignities

Section   3301(c)   Irretrievable Breakdown
                             Mutual Consent

Section   3301(d)   Irretrievable Breakdown
                             Two (2) Year Separation Where
                                 the Court Determines That
                                 There is a Reasonable Pros-
                                 pect of Reconciliation

A list of qualified professionals is available for inspection in the office of the Appointments Clerk of Family Court in B-16   or in the office of the Chief of the Domestic Relations Branch of the Family Court of Philadelphia, 34 S. 11th Street.

_____

Counsel for

5-174

223

INDEX

order. *See court*
order for shared custody, 116
order for temporary custody and support, 17
order of contempt, 100
order of court, 29, 91

P

parcel, 81
Parental Kidnapping Prevention Act, 100, 102, 103, 104
parenting time. *See visitation rights*
parents, 18, 20, 26, 27, 29, 31, 35, 37, 39, 51, 54, 58, 61, 62, 63, 65, 71, 72, 89, 95, 99, 116
    biological, 52
    custodial, 54, 59, 62, 65, 71, 97, 99, 116
    non-custodial, 51, 58, 59, 61, 62, 65, 72, 95, 99, 100, 116
    non-offending, 95
    offending, 95
    primary, 21
    rights, 39, 41
    step, 52
    unfit, 20, 21, 37
    unmarried, 39, 40, 41
partial custody. *See custody*
paternity, 25, 39–48, 58, 102
    acknowledgment, 44
    order, 45
    process, 44
    testing, 42, 43, 44, 45, 46
paternity order. *See paternity*
paternity testing. *See paternity*
Pennsylvania Digest, 115
Pennsylvania Divorce Code, 114
Pennsylvania Rules of Court, 115
perjury, 62
personal jurisdiction. *See jurisdiction*
petition for temporary custody, 80, 82, 89
petition to reduce child support. *See child support*
petitioner, 44, 69, 79, 90, 91, 94
physical custody. *See custody*
plaintiff. *See petitioner*
pleading, 104
practice manuals, 117
preference of the child, 18, 19, 22, 27, 37, 116
preliminary considerations, 1–8, 9–12, 13–14
primary parent. *See parents*
private school tuition, 65, 72
procedures, 5, 13, 64, 67, 75–86, 87–92, 93–98, 99–106, 112, 113, 115, 120, 121
process of paternity. *See paternity*
process server, 121
proof of service, 47
property, 4, 5, 25, 33, 38, 57, 62, 71, 88, 109

protection, 13, 25, 101, 102
prothonotary, 25, 69, 77, 78, 80, 81, 82, 87, 89, 91, 112, 114, 121
provision, 79
public policy, 35
Purdon's Pennsylvania Consolidated Statutes Annotated, 114

R

recipient, 73
referral service. *See attorney*
religion, 4, 18, 19, 23, 51
request for an adversarial hearing, 32, 54
request for hearing, 17
research, 114
residency, 9–12, 18, 19, 35, 63, 90, 103
respondent, 45, 46, 69, 79, 90
retroactivity. *See child support*
reverse of custody. *See custody*
rights of the father. *See father*
rights of the parents. *See parents*
Rules of Civil Procedure, 115
rules of procedure. *See court*

S

selecting an attorney. *See attorney*
separation, 3, 4, 6, 7, 11, 22, 23, 26, 28, 35, 58, 90, 101
service, 81
shared custody. *See custody*
sole custody. *See custody*
sole custody order, 116
special circumstances, 87–92
split custody. *See custody*
statutes, 40, 41, 42, 43, 44, 65, 94, 98, 114
step-parent. *See parents*
subject matter jurisdiction. *See jurisdiction*
subpoena, 34, 63
summer camp, 65
supervised visitation. *See visitation*
support. *See child support*
support counselor. *See child support*
support guideline computations-child support, 67
support officer. *See child support*

T

temporary custody. *See custody*
temporary jurisdiction. *See jurisdiction*
temporary order of court, 32
temporary relief, 104
testimony, 30, 32, 34
third-party visitation. *See visitation*
transportation, 31, 72
travel, 28
trial, 32, 45, 46

U

unfit parent. *See parents*
Uniform Child Custody Jurisdiction Act, 100, 101,
    102, 103, 104, 115
unmarried parents. *See parents*

V

vacation, 10, 28, 65
violation of custody, 91
visitation, 4, 5, 11, 13, 21, 22, 28, 39, 49–54, 57,
    58, 59, 78, 81, 84, 93–98, 99, 100, 102, 103,
    113
    agreement, 51, 52, 53
    balancing, 95
    compensatory, 95
    limitation, 51
    modification, 52
    order, 103, 116
    rights, 52, 54, 95, 103
    schedule, 52
    supervised, 51
    third-party, 102

W

waiver of the right to a hearing, 45
wedlock, 44
witness, 34, 43, 63

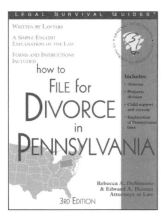

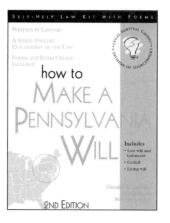

SPHINX® PUBLISHING'S NATIONAL TITLES
Valid in All 50 States

LEGAL SURVIVAL IN BUSINESS

The Complete Book of Corporate Forms	$24.95
How to Form a Delaware Corporation from Any State	$24.95
How to Form a Limited Liability Company	$22.95
Incorporate in Nevada from Any State	$24.95
How to Form a Nonprofit Corporation	$24.95
How to Form Your Own Corporation (3E)	$24.95
How to Form Your Own Partnership (2E)	$24.95
How to Register Your Own Copyright (4E)	$24.95
How to Register Your Own Trademark (3E)	$21.95
Most Valuable Business Legal Forms You'll Ever Need (3E)	$21.95

LEGAL SURVIVAL IN COURT

Crime Victim's Guide to Justice (2E)	$21.95
Grandparents' Rights (3E)	$24.95
Help Your Lawyer Win Your Case (2E)	$14.95
Jurors' Rights (2E)	$12.95
Legal Research Made Easy (3E)	$21.95
Winning Your Personal Injury Claim (2E)	$24.95
Your Rights When You Owe Too Much	$16.95

LEGAL SURVIVAL IN REAL ESTATE

Essential Guide to Real Estate Contracts	$18.95
Essential Guide to Real Estate Leases	$18.95
How to Buy a Condominium or Townhome (2E)	$19.95

LEGAL SURVIVAL IN PERSONAL AFFAIRS

Cómo Hacer su Propio Testamento	$16.95
Cómo Solicitar su Propio Divorcio	$24.95
Cómo Restablecer su propio Crédito y Renegociar sus Deudas	$21.95
Guía de Inmigración a Estados Unidos (3E)	$24.95
Guía de Justicia para Víctimas del Crimen	$21.95
The 529 College Savings Plan	$16.95
How to File Your Own Bankruptcy (5E)	$21.95
How to File Your Own Divorce (4E)	$24.95
How to Make Your Own Simple Will (3E)	$18.95
How to Write Your Own Living Will (2E)	$16.95
How to Write Your Own Premarital Agreement (3E)	$24.95
Living Trusts and Other Ways to Avoid Probate (3E)	$24.95
Manual de Beneficios para el Seguro Social	$18.95
Mastering the MBE	$16.95
Most Valuable Personal Legal Forms You'll Ever Need	$24.95
Neighbor v. Neighbor (2E)	$16.95
The Nanny and Domestic Help Legal Kit	$22.95
The Power of Attorney Handbook (4E)	$19.95
Repair Your Own Credit and Deal with Debt	$18.95
The Social Security Benefits Handbook (3E)	$18.95
Sexual Harassment:Your Guide to Legal Action	$18.95
Unmarried Parents' Rights	$19.95
U.S.A. Immigration Guide (3E)	$19.95
The Visitation Handbook	$18.95
Win Your Unemployment Compensation Claim (2E)	$21.95
Your Right to Child Custody, Visitation and Support (2E)	$24.95

Legal Survival Guides are directly available from Sourcebooks, Inc., or from your local bookstores.
Prices are subject to change without notice.

For credit card orders call 1–800–432–7444, write P.O. Box 4410, Naperville, IL 60567-4410
or fax 630-961-2168

Find more legal information at: **www.SphinxLegal.com**

SPHINX® PUBLISHING ORDER FORM

<table>
<tr><td colspan="2">BILL TO:</td><td colspan="2">SHIP TO:</td></tr>
<tr><td colspan="2"></td><td colspan="2"></td></tr>
<tr><td colspan="2"></td><td colspan="2"></td></tr>
<tr><td>Phone #</td><td>Terms</td><td>F.O.B.   Chicago, IL</td><td>Ship Date</td></tr>
</table>

Charge my: ☐ VISA ☐ MasterCard ☐ American Express

☐ **Money Order or Personal Check**

Credit Card Number   Expiration Date

Qty	ISBN	Title	Retail	Ext.
		SPHINX PUBLISHING NATIONAL TITLES		
	1-57248-148-X	Cómo Hacer su Propio Testamento	$16.95	
	1-57248-147-1	Cómo Solicitar su Propio Divorcio	$24.95	
	1-57248-226-5	Cómo Restablecer su propio Crédito y Renegociar sus Deudas	$21.95	
	1-57248-238-9	The 529 College Savings Plan	$16.95	
	1-57248-166-8	The Complete Book of Corporate Forms	$24.95	
	1-57248-163-3	Crime Victim's Guide to Justice (2E)	$21.95	
	1-57248-159-5	Essential Guide to Real Estate Contracts	$18.95	
	1-57248-160-9	Essential Guide to Real Estate Leases	$18.95	
	1-57248-139-0	Grandparents' Rights (3E)	$24.95	
	1-57248-188-9	Guía de Inmigración a Estados Unidos (3E)	$24.95	
	1-57248-187-0	Guía de Justicia para Víctimas del Crimen	$21.95	
	1-57248-103-X	Help Your Lawyer Win Your Case (2E)	$14.95	
	1-57248-164-1	How to Buy a Condominium or Townhome (2E)	$19.95	
	1-57248-191-9	How to File Your Own Bankruptcy (5E)	$21.95	
	1-57248-132-3	How to File Your Own Divorce (4E)	$24.95	
	1-57248-100-5	How to Form a DE Corporation from Any State	$24.95	
	1-57248-083-1	How to Form a Limited Liability Company	$22.95	
	1-57248-099-8	How to Form a Nonprofit Corporation	$24.95	
	1-57248-133-1	How to Form Your Own Corporation (3E)	$24.95	
	1-57248-224-9	How to Form Your Own Partnership (2E)	$24.95	
	1-57248-232-X	How to Make Your Own Simple Will (3E)	$18.95	
	1-57248-200-1	How to Register Your Own Copyright (4E)	$24.95	
	1-57248-104-8	How to Register Your Own Trademark (3E)	$21.95	
	1-57248-118-8	How to Write Your Own Living Will (2E)	$16.95	
	1-57248-156-0	How to Write Your Own Premarital Agreement (3E)	$24.95	
	1-57248-158-7	Incorporate in Nevada from Any State	$24.95	
	1-57071-333-2	Jurors' Rights (2E)	$12.95	
	1-57248-223-0	Legal Research Made Easy (3E)	$21.95	
	1-57248-165-X	Living Trusts and Other Ways to Avoid Probate (3E)	$24.95	
	1-57248-186-2	Manual de Beneficios para el Seguro Social	$18.95	

Qty	ISBN	Title	Retail	Ext.
	1-57248-220-6	Mastering the MBE	$16.95	
	1-57248-167-6	Most Valuable Bus. Legal Forms You'll Ever Need (3E)	$21.95	
	1-57248-130-7	Most Valuable Personal Legal Forms You'll Ever Need	$24.95	
	1-57248-098-X	The Nanny and Domestic Help Legal Kit	$22.95	
	1-57248-089-0	Neighbor v. Neighbor (2E)	$16.95	
	1-57248-169-2	The Power of Attorney Handbook (4E)	$19.95	
	1-57248-149-8	Repair Your Own Credit and Deal with Debt	$18.95	
	1-57248-217-6	Sexual Harassment: Your Guide to Legal Action	$18.95	
	1-57248-168-4	The Social Security Benefits Handbook (3E)	$18.95	
	1-57248-216-8	Social Security Q&A	$12.95	
	1-57071-399-5	Unmarried Parents' Rights	$19.95	
	1-57071-354-5	U.S.A. Immigration Guide (3E)	$19.95	
	1-57248-192-7	The Visitation Handbook	$18.95	
	1-57248-225-7	Win Your Unemployment Compensation Claim (2E)	$21.95	
	1-57248-138-2	Winning Your Personal Injury Claim (2E)	$24.95	
	1-57248-162-5	Your Right to Child Custody, Visitation and Support (2E)	$24.95	
	1-57248-157-9	Your Rights When You Owe Too Much	$16.95	
		CALIFORNIA TITLES		
	1-57248-150-1	CA Power of Attorney Handbook (2E)	$18.95	
	1-57248-151-X	How to File for Divorce in CA (3E)	$26.95	
	1-57071-356-1	How to Make a CA Will	$16.95	
	1-57248-145-5	How to Probate and Settle an Estate in California	$26.95	
	1-57248-146-3	How to Start a Business in CA	$18.95	
	1-57248-194-3	How to Win in Small Claims Court in CA (2E)	$18.95	
	1-57248-196-X	The Landlord's Legal Guide in CA	$24.95	
		FLORIDA TITLES		
	1-57071-363-4	Florida Power of Attorney Handbook (2E)	$16.95	
	1-57248-176-5	How to File for Divorce in FL (7E)	$26.95	
	1-57248-177-3	How to Form a Corporation in FL (5E)	$24.95	
	1-57248-203-6	How to Form a Limited Liability Co. in FL (2E)	$24.95	
	1-57071-401-0	How to Form a Partnership in FL	$22.95	

Form Continued on Following Page   **SUBTOTAL**

To order, call Sourcebooks at 1-800-432-7444 or FAX (630) 961-2168 (Bookstores, libraries, wholesalers—please call for discount)

Prices are subject to change without notice.

Find more legal information at: www.SphinxLegal.com

SPHINX® PUBLISHING ORDER FORM

Qty	ISBN	Title	Retail	Ext.
	1-57248-113-7	How to Make a FL Will (6E)	$16.95	
	1-57248-088-2	How to Modify Your FL Divorce Judgment (4E)	$24.95	
	1-57248-144-7	How to Probate and Settle an Estate in FL (4E)	$26.95	
	1-57248-081-5	How to Start a Business in FL (5E)	$16.95	
	1-57248-204-4	How to Win in Small Claims Court in FL (7E)	$18.95	
	1-57248-202-8	Land Trusts in Florida (6E)	$29.95	
	1-57248-123-4	Landlords' Rights and Duties in FL (8E)	$21.95	

GEORGIA TITLES

Qty	ISBN	Title	Retail	Ext.
	1-57248-137-4	How to File for Divorce in GA (4E)	$21.95	
	1-57248-180-3	How to Make a GA Will (4E)	$21.95	
	1-57248-140-4	How to Start a Business in Georgia (2E)	$16.95	

ILLINOIS TITLES

Qty	ISBN	Title	Retail	Ext.
	1-57071-405-3	How to File for Divorce in IL (2E)	$21.95	
	1-57248-170-6	How to Make an IL Will (3E)	$16.95	
	1-57071-416-9	How to Start a Business in IL (2E)	$18.95	
	1-57248-078-5	Landlords' Rights & Duties in IL	$21.95	

MASSACHUSETTS TITLES

Qty	ISBN	Title	Retail	Ext.
	1-57248-128-5	How to File for Divorce in MA (3E)	$24.95	
	1-57248-115-3	How to Form a Corporation in MA	$24.95	
	1-57248-108-0	How to Make a MA Will (2E)	$16.95	
	1-57248-106-4	How to Start a Business in MA (2E)	$18.95	
	1-57248-209-5	The Landlord's Legal Guide in MA	$24.95	

MICHIGAN TITLES

Qty	ISBN	Title	Retail	Ext.
	1-57248-215-X	How to File for Divorce in MI (3E)	$24.95	
	1-57248-182-X	How to Make a MI Will (3E)	$16.95	
	1-57248-183-8	How to Start a Business in MI (3E)	$18.95	

MINNESOTA TITLES

Qty	ISBN	Title	Retail	Ext.
	1-57248-142-0	How to File for Divorce in MN	$21.95	
	1-57248-179-X	How to Form a Corporation in MN	$24.95	
	1-57248-178-1	How to Make a MN Will (2E)	$16.95	

NEW YORK TITLES

Qty	ISBN	Title	Retail	Ext.
	1-57248-193-5	Child Custody, Visitation and Support in NY	$26.95	
	1-57248-141-2	How to File for Divorce in NY (2E)	$26.95	
	1-57248-105-6	How to Form a Corporation in NY	$24.95	
	1-57248-095-5	How to Make a NY Will (2E)	$16.95	
	1-57248-199-4	How to Start a Business in NY (2E)	$18.95	

Qty	ISBN	Title	Retail	Ext.
	1-57248-198-6	How to Win in Small Claims Court in NY (2E)	$18.95	
	1-57248-197-8	Landlords' Legal Guide in NY	$24.95	
	1-57071-188-7	New York Power of Attorney Handbook	$19.95	
	1-57248-122-6	Tenants' Rights in NY	$21.95	

NORTH CAROLINA TITLES

Qty	ISBN	Title	Retail	Ext.
	1-57248-185-4	How to File for Divorce in NC (3E)	$22.95	
	1-57248-129-3	How to Make a NC Will (3E)	$16.95	
	1-57248-184-6	How to Start a Business in NC (3E)	$18.95	
	1-57248-091-2	Landlords' Rights & Duties in NC	$21.95	

OHIO TITLES

Qty	ISBN	Title	Retail	Ext.
	1-57248-190-0	How to File for Divorce in OH (2E)	$24.95	
	1-57248-174-9	How to Form a Corporation in OH	$24.95	
	1-57248-173-0	How to Make an OH Will	$16.95	

PENNSYLVANIA TITLES

Qty	ISBN	Title	Retail	Ext.
	1-57248-242-7	Child Custody, Visitation and Support in Pennsylvania	$26.95	
	1-57248-211-7	How to File for Divorce in PA (3E)	$26.95	
	1-57248-094-7	How to Make a PA Will (2E)	$16.95	
	1-57248-112-9	How to Start a Business in PA (2E)	$18.95	
	1-57071-179-8	Landlords' Rights and Duties in PA	$19.95	

TEXAS TITLES

Qty	ISBN	Title	Retail	Ext.
	1-57248-171-4	Child Custody, Visitation, and Support in TX	$22.95	
	1-57248-172-2	How to File for Divorce in TX (3E)	$24.95	
	1-57248-114-5	How to Form a Corporation in TX (2E)	$24.95	
	1-57071-417-7	How to Make a TX Will (2E)	$16.95	
	1-57248-214-1	How to Probate and Settle an Estate in TX (3E)	$26.95	
	1-57248-228-1	How to Start a Business in TX (3E)	$18.95	
	1-57248-111-0	How to Win in Small Claims Court in TX (2E)	$16.95	
	1-57248-110-2	Landlords' Rights and Duties in TX (2E)	$21.95	

SUBTOTAL THIS PAGE _____

SUBTOTAL PREVIOUS PAGE _____

Shipping — $5.00 for 1st book, $1.00 each additional _____

Illinois residents add 6.75% sales tax _____

Connecticut residents add 6.00% sales tax _____

TOTAL _____

To order, call Sourcebooks at 1-800-432-7444 or FAX (630) 961-2168 (Bookstores, libraries, wholesalers—please call for discount)
Prices are subject to change without notice.
Find more legal information at: www.SphinxLegal.com